# The EVERYTHING®
## Cooking for Baby and Toddler

Dear Reader,

Thanks for picking up *The Everything® Cooking for Baby and Toddler Book!* Whether you're a new or experienced parent, you've probably thought about making your own baby food, but might not have known where to start. We were in just that situation.

When our daughter was a baby, we discovered that she couldn't tolerate many of the colorings, starches, and other additives in commercial baby food. We, the nervous first-time parents, were faced with the task of creating her meals from scratch instead of using the appealing little brightly colored jars from the grocery store.

After a few false starts (including a freezer full of cracked glass and hot sweet potatoes), we learned how to create tasty, healthy meals for her and our other children. We soon were hooked on the convenience and cost savings that come from customizing our child's diet exactly as we wished. We are pleased to share some of our children's favorite dishes with you, and hope that you will enjoy them as much as our family does.

Thanks again, and happy reading!

# The EVERYTHING® Series

## Editorial

| | |
|---|---|
| Publishing Director | Gary M. Krebs |
| Director of Product Development | Paula Munier |
| Associate Managing Editor | Laura M. Daly |
| Associate Copy Chief | Brett Palana-Shanahan |
| Acquisitions Editor | Kate Burgo |
| Development Editor | Rachel Engelson |
| Associate Production Editor | Casey Ebert |

## Production

| | |
|---|---|
| Director of Manufacturing | Susan Beale |
| Associate Director of Production | Michelle Roy Kelly |
| Series Designers | Daria Perreault |
| | Colleen Cunningham |
| Cover Design | Paul Beatrice |
| | Erick DaCosta |
| | Matt LeBlanc |
| Interior Layout | Heather Barrett |
| | Brewster Brownville |
| | Colleen Cunningham |
| | Jennifer Oliveira |
| Cover Artist and Interior Illustrator | Barry Littmann |

**Visit the entire Everything® Series at *www.everything.com***

# THE

# EVERYTHING®

# COOKING

## FOR BABY
## AND TODDLER
## BOOK

300 delicious, easy recipes to get
your child off to a healthy start

Shana Priwer and Cynthia Phillips

With technical review by Vincent Iannelli, M.D.

Adams Media
Avon, Massachusetts

To our children Zoecyn, Elijah, and Benjamin

An Everything® Series Book.
Everything® and everything.com® are registered trademarks of F+W Publications, Inc.

Published by Adams Media, an F+W Publications Company
57 Littlefield Street, Avon, MA 02322 U.S.A.
*www.adamsmedia.com*

ISBN 10: 1-59337-691-X
ISBN 13: 978-1-59337-691-8
Printed in the United States of America.

J   I   H   G   F   E   D   C   B   A

**Library of Congress Cataloging-in-Publication Data**
Priwer, Shana.
The everything cooking for baby and toddler book / Shana Priwer and Cynthia Phillips ;
With technical review by Vincent Iannelli.
p.          cm.
Includes index.
ISBN-13: 978-1-59337-691-8
ISBN-10: 1-59337-691-X
1.  Cookery (Baby foods) 2.  Infants--Nutrition. 3.  Toddlers--Nutrition.  I. Phillips, Cynthia. II. Title.
TX740.P76 2006
641.5'622--dc22
                2006028141

*This book is available at quantity discounts for bulk purchases.*
*For information, please call 1-800-289-0963.*

# Contents

# Acknowledgments

Special thanks to Dr. Marshall Gilula for his love and support, and to our children for taste testing these recipes.

# Introduction

Starting your baby on solid food can often seem like more of an art than a science. There's no "right" way to go about feeding, and you'll get helpful advice from your doctors, friends, and parents. The discouraging part is that most of what you'll hear will directly conflict with something else you've read or been told! This book will navigate these waters with sound, simple reasons for introducing or delaying some particular foods.

Remember, your baby's first foods don't have to be bland and boring, so forget about serving rice cereal at every meal. While grains are a wholesome part of a baby's diet, they don't need to be the staple of your young one's existence. You'll learn to make your own baby rice and baby oatmeal, but cooking for your baby goes far beyond these basics.

As you'll soon find out, cooking for your baby can be as simple or as complex as you want it to be. Many recipes in this cookbook require only one ingredient, which is exactly how it should be in the early days of your child's life—no one wants their baby eating strange preservatives with names too long to pronounce. This cookbook does away with all those "extras" and will teach you how to serve fresh, healthful meals every day of the week.

Any good cookbook will help you create a variety of meals. What's unique about this book is that everything is tailored to simple, healthful foods that can be prepared quickly and easily. No running to the market for some odd ingredient that's only grown in one tiny corner of the universe! With a few exceptions (such as homemade grape juice, soy milk, and yogurt), these recipes are easy, they make sense, and they can be fed to the entire family. Plus, you'll feel good about what you're feeding your growing baby!

In particular, this book includes recipes that are easily scalable so that you can make full-fledged meals for the rest of the family. Just take out a portion for your baby, then add spices and other flavorings to the rest of the meal to make it enjoyable for adult palates. These recipes may encourage your entire family to try flavor combinations or healthy ingredients that weren't part of your former cooking repertoire.

Also included are nutritional tips about why particular foods have been chosen or paired in the recipes. For example, some nutrients are better absorbed when taken in combination with other foods—vitamin D helps your body absorb calcium, for instance, and beans and rice together make a

complete protein. Some ingredients, such as parsnips or kiwi fruit, may seem exotic, but your baby doesn't know that! They're chock-full of vitamins and other nutrients. So try them, and you and your baby may discover a new favorite together.

It's important to get your baby used to eating a wide variety of foods, textures, and tastes in her first few years. Studies have shown that good, healthy eating habits need to start early. Many toddlers become picky when they reach two or three years old, but if you've had your child eating a wide range of foods, she'll be more likely to choose a few healthy ones later in life. Your child's first few years represent an important window of opportunity to establish healthy patterns that can help sustain your child for the rest of her life. So get that food processor ready, and prepare to purée!

# part 1

# Introduction to Feeding

**W**elcome to the wonderful world of baby food! Babies have a number of important milestones in their first year. Smiling, giggling, sitting up, crawling, walking, and taking that first mouthful of solid food are achievements that contribute to your baby's growing independence. New parents are especially infatuated with their baby's first foods because, after all, eating is fun! We love to eat, and so do our children. Creating meals that both nourish and please is highly satisfying for all involved.

# Why Homemade?

While jarred food and boxes of baby cereal have their place, the focus of this book is on homemade baby food. Why make your own baby food when so much is made for you, sold in supermarkets, and is ready to go? For starters, try convenience! Rice cereal must be mixed with water, breastmilk, or formula, and can't be stored once you've mixed it. Store-bought baby foods are often several servings' worth for young babies, and can't be stored if you feed directly out of the jar.

Those cute little jars of baby food you see on the supermarket shelves will also leave a not-so-cute dent in your wallet. Jarred baby food is more expensive than homemade, particularly for large inexpensive vegetables such as sweet potatoes. For the price of a single large sweet potato (which might make 4–8 jars' worth), you could purchase only one or two jars of the store version. Doing it yourself will save money almost every time.

And don't forget about taste. Store-bought foods often taste like they've been sitting around for a while, and their flavors are flat. Babies know the difference! Nutrition is also a concern. While single-ingredient jarred baby foods are made without preservatives or spices, most fresh fruits and vegetables will lose some of their vitamins during the jarring process. Fresh homemade purées are the best thing you can feed young babies because they retain the vitamins and minerals.

Finally, you know what's in the food that you prepare. You never have to worry about salt, sugar, or any other mysterious ingredients that might go into your child's delicate stomach. You have complete control over what you feed your baby when making your own food, and you can tailor your recipes to your baby's developing preferences.

# First Foods

One of the most common questions about feeding young babies is what to offer first. Typically, the first foods include cereals, single fruits, and single vegetables. It's important to wait a few days between new foods; you'll want to make sure your baby does not develop any sort of allergic reaction before offering more foods that are new. Cereals are the least likely to spark an allergic reaction, so they're usually a safe first food.

Be sure to avoid anything with wheat and eggs for the first six months, as both are common allergens. Avoid egg whites until an infant is one year old. Honey should also be avoided until your baby is at least a year old, because it can contain a dangerous botulism spore. If your family has any history of allergy to nuts, avoid peanuts or any products with tree nuts until your child is at least three years old. Without a family history of peanut or tree nut allergies, it's relatively safe to introduce nut butters from about twelve months on. Experts usually recommend that parents avoid nuts and other "allergic"foods if their baby has any of these risk factors:

1. The infant already has an allergy to another food
2. The infant has other "allergic" type disorders, such as eczema, asthma, or hay fever
3. The infant has family members with food allergies, eczema, allergies, or asthma

Remember that the goal of feeding in the first year is mostly about getting your baby used to different tastes and textures. Breastmilk or formula will still provide most of the calories and other nutrients to your baby's diet through the first year.

## Tools of the Trade

While some baby foods can be made with nothing more than the silverware you already have, others require more in the way of equipment. Very ripe fruits, such as avocados, bananas, and pears, can be mashed with a fork. That's it! They don't require cooking or puréeing.

For the meat-and-vegetable purées, or any of the more complex recipes for younger babies, you'll need more than a fork. Consider purchasing a food processor, blender, food mill, "mini" chopper, or other machine that will grind and pulse your food into a purée. These tools range dramatically in price and capacity, so choose accordingly based on your needs. Do you plan to make only enough food for one or two servings at a time? If so, go with a smaller model. If you want to make a month's worth, consider a full-sized food processor.

Thicker purées usually can be thinned with water but, even so, some may have too grainy a texture. Use a food strainer (or even a colander) to further thin your purées before serving. Another very useful tool is a mortar and pestle—rice, oats, and other grains can be ground to a powder quickly and easily, especially for small amounts.

When it comes time to feed your baby, consider using coated spoons. These are small baby-sized spoons that have plastic or rubber tips. They're available in stores, inexpensive, and perfect for your baby's sensitive mouth. Many of these spoons are heat-sensitive, and will quickly change colors to warn you if the food you're about to serve is too hot.

## Storing Baby Food

Now that you're on the road to preparing all of your baby's meals, you'll want to make sure that you store future servings in a safe way. There are several options. Some families stock up on freezer-safe glass jars and lids, and freeze a container's worth at a time. This technique works well, as long as you remember to let the food cool before freezing. Also, don't fill the jars up to the rim because the food will expand as it freezes. Plastic freezer containers will also work, but look for smaller containers. You can recycle commercial baby food jars for freezing, but because they weren't designed to be frozen, they may explode in the freezer. Freezer-safe glass or plastic is the best for this storage.

Another popular technique is to freeze baby food in ice-cube trays. This allows for single-serving storage, which is a great idea for babies who don't consume very much at one sitting. Look for ice-cube trays with covers; if unavailable, wrap the ice-cube tray in plastic wrap before storing. Once the food is frozen, you can tip out the baby-food cubes into a plastic freezer bag, remove, and thaw one cube at a time.

Always label your baby food with the ingredients and date of storage. Most homemade baby foods will keep in the freezer for about three months, so be sure to rotate through your older stock as you add new meals to the freezer. Once you've thawed a container of baby food and are storing it in the refrigerator, use it within a day or two.

Generally, baby food is safe to serve if it has freezer burn. Freezer burn results when extra air gets into the food. It is different from the ice crystals that often appear on baby food. These crystals result from all the liquid in most baby foods. The icy or frozen part of the food will taste drier than the rest, but it can be removed before heating.

Frozen baby food can be thawed in any number of ways. Most foods will thaw in the refrigerator within about four hours, and this is one of the safer methods. Never leave baby food out on the counter to thaw, especially if it contains meat, because it may gather bacteria and become unsafe. Baby food can be thawed in a saucepan on the stove, or in the microwave, but stir frequently, and be sure to test the temperature before serving. Once you've thawed a container of baby food, don't refreeze it unless you've cooked it first.

## A Word of Caution

Once you've gotten the hang of making baby food, it may be tempting to start puréeing everything in sight. And, once your baby is about one year old, you can serve him most of the same foods that you would consume. However, there are a few items that you should either wait on, or purchase pre-made.

Root vegetables (carrots, beets, turnips) and leafy green vegetables (spinach, lettuce, collard greens) can contain more nitrates than most other vegetables. This is mostly because these vegetables have more exposure to soil and ground water. Excess nitrates in young babies can lead to problems with their oxygen saturation, a rare but potentially fatal problem. Because of the high concentration of nitrates in these vegetables, it's best to wait either until your baby is seven or eight months old, or use commercially prepared versions if you want to feed them to your baby. Commercial baby food manufacturers can screen for nitrate levels in their vegetables, but this screening can't be done at home. If you choose to make your own versions of these foods earlier than eight months, avoid using the cooking water as a liquid thinner (since it will contain additional nitrates) and use organic vegetables, which aren't grown in nitrate fertilizer.

Once your toddler starts eating "chewing foods," or ones that require a few more teeth, you will also need to be very aware of choking hazards. Foods such as hot dogs, grapes, peanuts, and popcorn are dangerous for children who do not yet chew their food thoroughly, and these should be avoided altogether or fed to a child only under close supervision.

## Tackling Texture

Another common question of parents of young eaters: how creamy does their food need to be? While most six-month-olds are still content to eat food that has been 100 percent puréed, some (especially early teethers) will be ready for more textured food. Around six or seven months, try offering foods that haven't been puréed into submission; pulse the food processor enough to grind up the meal, but leave it slightly coarser. Experiment with what your baby will tolerate. If your baby closes her mouth or appears to gag on every bite, go back to the smoother foods for a few days.

Gradually start introducing more discrete bites of food. Biter biscuits, teething crackers, and other melt away–style foods will help your baby gain confidence and also help her get used to swallowing food with texture. She'll eventually get used to the "Stage 3"–style meals that you prepare for her, which will include purées mixed with some lumpier textures.

Some babies even jump straight to the real thing! If your child expresses no interest in lumpier textures, try offering small bites of the genuine article. Sweet potatoes can be fork-mashed and picked up by little fingers, and some babies will prefer self-feeding at a very early age. Look to your child for cues as to how to prepare her meals.

## Baby Nutrition

When your baby is exclusively breast- or formula-fed, you know that he's getting enough of what he needs. What about once he starts solids? Do you need to start calculating how many grams of protein he's consuming every day? What about iron and calcium?

The short answer: don't worry too much. Most of a baby's nutrition in the first six or seven months will be coming from breastmilk or formula. Up through the first year, a little more than half of a baby's calories and other nutrition will still be in liquid form; solid food will make up about half of a baby's calories. The purposes of solid foods during the first year are to help your baby get used to the texture of solid food, enhance his hand-eye coordination as he learns to get food into his mouth, and provide him with calories and vitamins (iron, etc.). Continue breast- or formula-feeding as necessary, and let your baby's appetite dictate his feeding schedule.

## Nutrition Requirements:

Up to 6 months: 35–55 kcal/pound (a 15-lb baby would require 525–800 calories a day)

0–6 months 49 kcal/pound (about 650 calories a day)

6–12 months 45 kcal/pound (about 850 calories a day)

1–3 years 46 kcal/pound (about 1,300 calories a day)

# A No-Frills Diet

The world of food is brand-new to your baby, and she's easily impressed by the simplest of choices. Fruits and vegetables are naturally sweet, and baby food never requires salt, sugar, or other spices. Avoid packaged cookies, crackers, or other snacks that contain these unnecessary ingredients. There's no reason to give your baby an artificial sweet tooth!

It's also a good idea to skip the bacon and sausage. Babies don't need processed foods, which are difficult to digest and may cause upset stomachs. Stick to simple and natural foods, avoiding anything greasy or full of spices. In other words, feed your baby the way that you *should* feed yourself!

Some parents, seeing their baby's chubby cheeks and thighs, feed their babies low- or even nonfat yogurt. This is a mistake. Lower-fat dairy products should not be given until your child is at least two years old (and nonfat products should be avoided until your child is closer to five years old). Fat is necessary for proper brain development, and the extra calories are necessary to supplement the baby's diet. The American Academy of Pediatrics recommends that babies get approximately half their calories from fat; this amount decreases to one-third of their daily requirement after they reach two years of age. It is therefore a good idea to feed your baby whole milk after one year, if a mother is no longer breastfeeding, and try whole-fat yogurt and cheese after nine months.

Setting out to prepare your baby's food from fresh, organic produce is a wonderful ambition. You'll rest assured that your baby is getting the most nutritious food she could possibly have. Don't get discouraged, though, if you end up substituting. Not all vegetables are available year-round, and most of the time it's perfectly healthful to use frozen produce instead. Take advantage of what's seasonally available, exercise care in food preparation and storage, and be proud of your accomplishment!

# 4–6 Months

¼ cup white or brown rice
1 cup water

# Simple Rice Cereal

*Rice cereal is one of the most common first foods for babies. It is
easy to digest, sits well, and doesn't carry the allergenic potential of
other wheat-based cereals because it is gluten free. Make enough for
your little one, or prepare a larger serving for the older children!*

* * * * *

1. Grind rice into a powder, using either a food processor or blender.

2. Pour water into a small saucepan. Bring to a rolling boil.

3. Add the rice powder into the boiling water, stirring constantly for about 30 seconds.

4. Cover the pot, turn the heat down to low, and simmer for 7–8 minutes, or until the rice is a smooth, thick consistency. Stir occasionally to prevent sticking.

5. Let cool to lukewarm. Thin with breastmilk or formula to desired consistency. For a baby just starting solids, the cereal should be thin and run off the spoon easily.

### Baby's First Foods

*Rice, oatmeal, barley, and corn are all excellent grains that can be
prepared into cereals. Beware, though, of cereals that may contain
wheat. As a common allergen, wheat should not be introduced into
your baby's diet until she's about 1 year old. Without risk factors,
cereals including wheat can be introduced by 6–8 months.*

# Simple Oatmeal Cereal

**1–2 Servings**

¼ cup regular oats (not
    quick-cooking)
1 cup water

*Oatmeal is a great early cereal, and has a taste many babies love. A note on quantities: ¼ cup of oats may be difficult to purée in a full-size food processor. Use a mini-grinder when making small amounts, or make a larger amount of oatmeal, and store the extra. Keep it tightly sealed, and it will last for 1–2 weeks.*

•   •   •   •   •

1. Grind oats into a powder, using either a food processor or blender. Alternatively, a mortar and pestle make a terrific grinder for a small amount.

2. Pour the water into a small saucepan. Bring to a rolling boil.

3. Add the powdered oats into the boiling water, stirring constantly for about 30 seconds.

4. Cover the pot, turn the heat down to low, and simmer for 8–10 minutes, or until the oats are smooth and thick. Stir occasionally to prevent sticking and burning.

5. Let cool to lukewarm. Thin with breastmilk or formula to desired consistency.

### Safe Leftovers

*Always put a small amount of food into a separate dish to feed your baby. With this recipe, for example, don't pour all of the oatmeal into one dish. Once the baby's spoon has gone from his mouth back into the dish, the leftovers can't be safely stored. Try putting one tablespoon of oatmeal into a bowl to start.*

*¼ cup barley*
*1 cup water*

# Simple Barley Cereal

*Barley has a slightly stronger flavor than rice or oatmeal. For this reason, try introducing it after your baby is already accustomed to other cereals. Barley also tends to be thicker than oatmeal or rice, so thin with extra water, formula, or breastmilk if necessary.*

* * * * *

1. Grind barley into a powder, using either a food processor or blender.

2. Pour water into a small saucepan. Bring to a rolling boil.

3. Add ground barley into the boiling water, stirring constantly for about 30 seconds.

4. Cover the pot, turn the heat down to low, and simmer for 8–10 minutes. Stir to prevent sticking.

5. Let cool to lukewarm. Thin with breastmilk or formula to desired consistency.

### Cereal Temperature
*Homemade baby cereal will be hot off the stove. Let the cereal cool to just above room temperature before serving. Some babies prefer their cereal cold, so you might want to refrigerate it first, or add a little cold water.*

# Puréed Green Beans

**4 Servings**

*1 cup green beans*
*2 tablespoons water*

*If green beans aren't in season, you can substitute frozen beans in this recipe. Cook according to the directions on the package before puréeing. Make sure to purchase beans without added salt or other spices. Stay away from canned beans, because they often have added salt and they lose nutritional value in the canning process.*

• • • • •

1. Wash beans and break off ends, and break in half. Put them into a steamer basket, or place in a saucepan covered by an inch of water. Cover.

2. Heat to a boil, then turn down heat slightly. Steam until tender, about 5 minutes.

3. Place the beans into a food processor or blender. Purée to a chunky consistency.

4. Add the leftover water from steaming, 1 tablespoon at a time, to the green beans. If there isn't any water left, add water, breastmilk, or formula.

5. Continue puréeing until smooth.

**4 Servings**

½ cup fresh or frozen peas
2 tablespoons water

# Puréed Peas

*After shelling, a pound of fresh peas yields about 1 cup. Preparing fresh peas can take quite a while, and may be more labor-intensive than you had in mind. Depending on location and time of year, it may be more cost-effective to use frozen peas, and they'll contain most of the same nutrients.*

* * * * *

1. Put the peas into a steamer basket, or place into a saucepan covered by 1 inch of water. Steam the peas until tender, about 10–12 minutes.

2. Drain the peas and place into a food processor or blender. Purée to a chunky consistency.

3. Add leftover water from steaming, using 1 tablespoon at a time. Otherwise, add water, breastmilk, or formula.

4. Continue puréeing until smooth.

### Safe Storage
*Freshly puréed vegetables will keep in the refrigerator for 2–3 days. Store them in a tightly sealed container, and always serve your baby from a separate bowl. Peas may thicken after refrigeration, so add a bit of water or formula, and stir well before serving.*

# Applesauce

*Applesauce is a great recipe to double, triple, or quadruple. Homemade applesauce is a favorite food for children of all ages, and it's so versatile! Red Delicious, Braeburn, and Gala apples make particularly good applesauce, though almost any variety can be used.*

**4 Servings**

*1 apple*
*½ cup water*

•  •  •  •  •

1. Wash the apple thoroughly, removing any bruised parts. Peel, core, and slice the apple into small pieces.

2. Cover with water in a saucepan. Cover pot and steam until tender, stirring occasionally, about 6–8 minutes.

3. Place apples into food processor or blender. Purée until chunky.

4. Add leftover boiling water 1 tablespoon at a time, and purée until smooth.

5. If the mixture is too coarse, pass through a fine sieve before serving and storing.

**Fiber First**
*One of the best things about applesauce is it's a great way to incorporate fiber into your child's diet. Apples contain both soluble and insoluble fiber, in addition to being a great source of vitamins and minerals. For older babies, use applesauce as a topping, or replace oil with applesauce when baking.*

1 peach
¼ cup water

# Peach Sauce

*When making recipes like this peach sauce, keep in mind that, especially when they first begin eating solid foods, babies won't consume very much at a time. A 6-month-old may eat 1–2 tablespoons of puréed fruit at a sitting. As babies gain more experience with the sensations and textures of solids, amounts will double and then triple. Start out small, and offer as much as your baby seems to want.*

1. Wash the peach thoroughly. Prick all over with a fork. Cut in half and place face-down in a shallow pan of water. Bring to a boil and steam until tender.

2. Peel off skin and remove pit.

3. Place peach into food processor or blender. Purée for 30 seconds.

4. Add leftover boiling water 1 tablespoon at a time, and purée until smooth.

5. If the mixture is too coarse, pass it through a fine sieve before serving and storing.

### Peach Sack

*Teething troubles starting to get your baby down? Try frozen peach slices placed into a mesh baby-feeder sack. The coldness will soothe baby's gums, but it'll taste a lot better than a frozen teether! You can also use fresh peach slices in the feeder sack for a juicier tasting experience.*

# Plum Sauce

**2 Servings**

*1 plum*
*¼ cup water*

*Picking a good plum is the most important part of this recipe. Make sure you get one that's already ripe; it should yield to the touch when you press it. Unripe plums won't steam properly and, as a result, will be too coarse when puréed. They also won't be as sweet as your baby might like!*

•   •   •   •   •

1. Wash the plum thoroughly. Peel, remove the pit, and cut into quarters.

2. Place in a steaming basket over water. Cover and steam until very tender.

3. Place plum into food processor or blender. Purée for 30 seconds.

4. Add leftover boiling water 1 tablespoon at a time, and purée until smooth.

5. If the mixture is too coarse, pass it through a fine sieve before serving and storing.

## Baby Food Thinners
*Most puréed baby foods will start out too thick for your little one to swallow. Generally, you can thin any purée with leftover boiled water. You can also thin cereals with formula or breastmilk, because they will provide extra nutrients. Always use fresh milk or formula; don't use leftover milk from your baby's bottle, since bacteria may already be introduced.*

*1 small fresh pear*
*¼ cup water*

# Pear Sauce

*Pears are very sweet, and most babies like them right off the bat. Look for a ripe pear with a good fragrance—the fruit should yield just slightly to the touch. You can buy unripe pears and let them ripen on your counter for a few days. Be sure to check them often because once they ripen, they can rot very quickly.*

●　●　●　●　●

1. Wash the pear thoroughly. Cut out any damaged sections.

2. Peel, core, and cut the pear into sections. If a vegetable peeler removes too much of the fruit, try scraping the peel away gently with a paring knife.

3. Place a steaming basket inside a small saucepan. Add enough water to cover the bottom of the pan, up to the level of the bottom of the steamer. Put the pear pieces into the basket, and steam until very tender.

4. Place pears into food processor or blender. Purée for 30 seconds.

5. Add leftover boiling water 1 tablespoon at a time, and purée until smooth.

### Tools of the Trade

*For many puréed recipes, you'll need a food processor or blender to achieve a smooth, thin texture that a baby will tolerate. Some fruits, though, are inherently less coarse than others. Pears, for example, can often be fork-mashed after steaming. With a very ripe pear, you may be able to fork-mash it raw and forgo the steaming altogether!*

# Puréed Sweet Potatoes

**4 Servings**

*½ sweet potato*
*½ cup water*

*Potatoes are easy for most babies to digest, and are a favorite first food. They are also easy to keep on hand, because they last longer than fruit and other vegetables.*

* * * * *

1. Bake the sweet potato at 400°F for 40 minutes, or cut into chunks and boil until tender.

2. Remove the skin and cut into small pieces.

3. Place into food processor or blender, and purée until smooth.

4. Add leftover boiling water, breastmilk, or formula. Purée until thin and creamy.

5. For older babies, use less water to create a chunkier consistency.

½ small winter squash
½ cup water

# Puréed Winter Squash

*Most babies love the sweet, smooth consistency of puréed squash.*
*Acorn and butternut are two main varieties.*

*     *     *     *     *

1. Scoop the seeds out of the squash. Cut into large pieces.

2. Steam until tender. Scoop cooked squash out of peel.

3. Place squash in food processor or blender, and purée until it is a stringy consistency.

4. Add leftover boiling water, breastmilk, or formula. Continue puréeing until smooth.

### Sweet Potatoes or Yams?
*Yams and sweet potatoes are different vegetables, but babies won't be able to tell them apart. Yams are usually slightly sweeter, but sweet potatoes contain more vitamin A and vitamin C. Unless you have a strong preference, go with whatever is available in your local market.*

# 6–9 Months

# Puréed Chicken

*When dealing with raw poultry, it is especially important to keep your workspace clean and sanitary. Scrub all work surfaces with hot soapy water, wash your hands, and use a disinfectant wipe to clean your cutting surface. Thoroughly clean all cutting utensils, never serve meat that is not completely cooked, and avoid cross contaminating things.*

* * * * *

**4 Servings**

*4 ounces of boneless chicken breast (about one small breast)*

*4 tablespoons chicken broth, breastmilk, or formula*

1. Remove fat and skin from chicken.

2. Place in a saucepan with a small amount of water, enough to almost cover the chicken. Cook over medium heat until completely cooked through, about 10 minutes.

3. Cut into small pieces and place in food processor or blender. Purée for about 30 seconds.

4. Add broth or formula, 1 tablespoon at a time. Continue puréeing until smooth.

### Sharing the Family Meal
*If you're making chicken for the family, save some for older babies, too! Roasted chicken has a tender consistency that's perfect for them. You may not even have to purée it—just take a small piece of the tender meat, remove the skin, and mash it with your fingers before feeding it to your baby.*

**2 Servings**

½ cup cooked ham
3 tablespoons water,
     breastmilk, or formula

# Puréed Ham

*Ham can be a tasty meal, but it should be served in small quantities until your baby approaches her first birthday. Salted cured meats are high in nitrates and sodium. However, it's a new taste that many babies enjoy, and exposing babies to foods of varying flavors will encourage their future culinary experimentation.*

·  ·  ·  ·  ·

1. Chop precooked ham into small pieces.

2. Place in food processor or blender. Purée for about 30 seconds.

3. Add water or formula, 1 tablespoon at a time. Continue puréeing until smooth.

### Combo Meals

*Most puréed meats can be easily combined with fruits and vegetables to create a healthy meal. Ham, for example, goes well with peas, so make a ham and pea purée. Don't be afraid to experiment, as long as your baby has had all the ingredients separately on previous occasions (and has shown no allergies to any of them).*

# Puréed Beef

**2 Servings**

*4 ounces of lean beef*
*3 tablespoons water,*
*   breastmilk, or formula*

*You don't need to purchase filet mignon for your baby, but don't use the cheapest cut you can find, either. Very tough meat will become grainy when cooked, and pasty when puréed. Rib roast and short loin are both tender cuts that will purée nicely. Stick to leaner cuts (less than 10 grams of fat per 100 grams of beef).*

●　　●　　●　　●　　●

1. Brown the beef in a pan until completely cooked through, typically 4–5 minutes per side for a thin steak. For a thicker piece, grill or roast until the interior temperature reaches 170°F.

2. Cut into small pieces and place in a food processor or blender. Purée for about 30 seconds, until the meat becomes a chunky powder.

3. Add water or formula, 1 tablespoon at a time. Continue puréeing until smooth.

### Beef Preparation
*Frozen beef can be safely thawed in the refrigerator or microwave. Raw beef may contain* E. coli, *salmonella,* Staphylococcus aureus *or* Listeria monocytogenes, *so take care with the cooking and cleanup. Cook the meat thoroughly in order to destroy bacteria. Use beef to make baby food within 2 hours of cooking and refrigerate if you don't plan to use the meat right away.*

½ *cup turkey*
*3 tablespoons turkey broth,*
*breastmilk, or formula*

# Puréed Turkey

*This is a great dish to make after Thanksgiving with leftover turkey. Dark meat has a gamier taste that may not appeal to some babies, so try using leftover white meat instead. Use moist, tender meat—dry turkey takes on a pasty texture when puréed. If using cooked leftover turkey, just skip ahead to the puréeing step.*

* * * * *

1. Remove fat and skin from turkey.

2. Place in a saucepan with a small amount of water. Cook over medium heat until completely cooked.

3. Cut into small pieces and place in a food processor or blender. Purée for about 30 seconds.

4. Add broth or milk, 1 tablespoon at a time. Continue puréeing until smooth.

### Steam It or Grill It?

*If your baby is older than 6 or 7 months, consider grilling meat instead of steaming it before you purée it. Grill a turkey breast in a pan, adding a bit of butter and onion for flavor. Make sure your baby has had these extra seasonings before, though.*

# Puréed Veal

*Veal comes from smaller, younger cows than beef does. These cows are usually milk-fed (as opposed to corn-fed, for the organically conscious), but they might be grass-fed as well. Veal is higher in cholesterol than beef, and pinker in color. Your baby isn't likely to prefer one over the other at this age, but the flavor is typically milder than beef.*

* * * * *

1. Cook the onion over medium heat until translucent.

2. Add veal to the pan and fry until completely cooked, typically 4–5 minutes per side for a thin steak.

3. Cut into small pieces (less than 1 inch square) and place in a food processor or blender. Purée for about 30 seconds, until the meat becomes a chunky powder.

4. Add water or milk, 1 tablespoon at a time. Continue puréeing until smooth.

### Flavoring a Simple Meat Purée
*The first time your baby is exposed to meats, make the meal as simple as possible: puréed meat, water or milk, and nothing more. Once your baby is used to the texture and taste, though, feel free to start experimenting! Sautéing the meat with onion or celery is a quick way to add flavor.*

**2 Servings**

1 tablespoon onion, minced
4 ounces of lean veal
3 tablespoons water,
    breastmilk, or formula

## Puréed Lamb

**2 Servings**

4 ounces of lean lamb
3 tablespoons water,
   breastmilk, or formula

*Lamb is easily digested by most babies older than 6 months, and presents yet another new flavor that you're not likely to find in jarred baby food. Babies start needing more iron in their diet around this age, and lamb is an excellent source of iron.*

· · · · ·

1. If using lamb chops, broil for 18–20 minutes, or until the meat reaches an internal temperature of 160°F. If using lamb shoulder or leg, roast at 325° F for 35–40 minutes.

2. Let the meat cool; then cut into small pieces and place in food processor or blender. Purée for about 30 seconds, until the meat becomes a chunky powder.

3. Add water or milk, 1 tablespoon at a time. Continue puréeing until smooth.

## Mashed Banana

**1 Serving**

1 very ripe banana

*Mashed bananas are one of the simplest foods you can prepare for your baby. No equipment (other than a fork) is required! Bananas tend to constipate, though, so be careful.*

· · · · ·

1. Slice off and peel about 1 inch of banana, removing any strings.

2. Mash with a fork until smooth.

# Mashed Avocado

**1 Serving**

*1 very ripe avocado*

*Avocado is a great first food. It's loaded with monounsaturated fat (the good-for-you kind), folate, potassium, and fiber. Avocados even contain a little protein, and are a great addition to your baby's diet. Avocados do have more calories than other fruits and vegetables, so use this recipe in moderation.*

•   •   •   •   •

1.  Cut a slice of avocado about ½ inch thick. Scoop avocado flesh from skin.

2.  Mash with a fork until smooth.

3.  If needed, add a little formula or breastmilk for a creamier texture.

### Make It a Meal
*A fantastic mixed dish is mashed bananas and avocados. Start with about 1 inch of ripe banana and a ½-inch slice of ripe avocado. Fork-mash with about 2 tablespoons of breastmilk or formula, and you'll have a meal that's sure to please.*

**3 Servings**
_____

1 cup fresh carrots (2
    medium-sized carrots)
¼ cup water

# Puréed Carrots

*Some vegetables, including carrots, may leak nitrates into the cooking
water as they're boiled. For this reason, babies younger than 7 months
should not eat homemade puréed carrots. As an extra precaution, do not
use the cooking water when thinning out this purée.*

●   ●   ●   ●   ●

1. Wash and peel the carrots. Cut into small pieces.

2. Place into a saucepan with enough water to cover the carrots. Bring the water
   to a boil; then simmer until the carrots are very tender, 15–20 minutes.

3. Drain the carrots and place into a blender or food processor. Purée for
   about 30 seconds.

4. Add in the water. Continue puréeing until smooth. Yield should be
   about ¾ cup, or 3 servings.

**3 Servings**
_____

1 cup broccoli
2 cups water

# Puréed Broccoli

*Broccoli is a terrific food for babies, because it is packed with vitamin
C, potassium, and folate. Try serving broccoli and cauliflower
together for babies more than 8 months old.*

●   ●   ●   ●   ●

1. Wash the broccoli. Chop off the stems and leaves and cut the florets
   into small pieces.

2. Put into a steamer basket. Bring to a boil and steam until tender, about
   15 minutes.

3. Place into a food processor or blender, and purée for about 30 seconds.
   Add liquid as necessary to achieve desired consistency.

# Puréed Cauliflower

**3 Servings**

*1 cup cauliflower*
*2 cups water*

*Cauliflower contains many cancer-fighting nutrients, so start
your baby off on the right foot with this tasty recipe!*

●　●　●　●　●

1. Wash the cauliflower thoroughly. Discard the stem and leaves and chop the florets into small pieces.

2. Put into a steamer basket. Bring to a boil and steam until tender, about 20 minutes.

3. Place into a food processor or blender, and purée for 30 seconds. Add liquid as necessary to achieve desired consistency.

### To Stem or Not to Stem?
*With vegetables such as broccoli and cauliflower, most adults cook and consume both the stems and the florets. When puréeing for a young baby, though, the purée will be smoother if you omit the tough stems.*

**6 Servings**

1 medium-sized white
    potato
½ small onion, optional
butter, optional
½ cup water
1 cup fresh or frozen
    spinach

# Spinach and Potatoes

*As with carrots, spinach may contain naturally occurring nitrates and should only be given to babies older than 7 months. Even then, use in moderation until your baby is closer to 1 year old. For this recipe, you could substitute commercially prepared jarred baby spinach, which is free of nitrates.*

⊙  ⊙  ⊙  ⊙  ⊙

1.  Wash and peel the potato. Cut it into small pieces.

2.  Peel and slice the onion into thin pieces. Sauté in a deep nonstick pan until soft and translucent. If the onion sticks, use some butter in the pan. Avoid using cooking oil.

3.  Add the diced potato and water to the pan. Bring to a boil; then turn down the heat and simmer until the potato is tender, about 25–30 minutes. Add more water if the potato sticks to the pan.

4.  If using fresh spinach, wash the leaves thoroughly, chop, and remove all stems. Boil in a pan of shallow water for about 10 minutes. If using frozen spinach, defrost and cook according to the package directions.

5.  Combine the cooked potatoes, onion, and spinach in a food processor or blender. Purée until smooth, adding liquid as needed to achieve the desired consistency.

# Carrot and Rice Purée

**3 Servings**

½ cup fresh carrots (1 medium-sized carrot)
2 tablespoons white or brown rice
¾ cup water

*Carrots and rice are a great mixed purée. Your baby will love the sweetness of the carrots combined with the nuttier flavor of the rice. Almost any type of rice will work in this recipe except those that stay hard even when cooked, such as wild rice. Also, sweet rice is sticky, and may be more difficult to purée.*

•  •  •  •  •

1.  Wash and peel the carrot. Cut into 1-inch pieces.

2.  Wash the rice to remove any dirt. Place into a medium saucepan, along with the carrots.

3.  Add enough water to cover the rice and carrots. Bring to a boil.

4.  Reduce the heat to low. Cover the saucepan and simmer until most of the water is absorbed, about 35–40 minutes.

5.  Place into a food processor or blender. Purée until smooth. Add liquid if necessary.

### Cooking for the Week
*With most of the puréed recipes in this book, you can always double or triple the ingredients to make a larger amount. Generally speaking, puréed vegetables made with water will keep in the refrigerator for 1–2 days. Freeze the extra in small containers or ice-cube trays.*

**4 Servings**

*1 cup fresh carrots
(2 medium-sized carrots)
1 cup fresh parsnip (about
1 small parsnip)
2 cups water*

# Carrot and Parsnip Purée

*This sweet dish will encourage your baby's love of vegetables. Parsnips are a less-common first food for babies, but they're loaded with potassium, fiber, vitamin C, and vitamin A. They even contain a little protein! They're found most readily in the winter, but should be available nearly all year round.*

* * * * *

1. Wash and peel the carrots. Cut into 1-inch pieces.

2. Wash and peel the parsnip. Cut into small chunks.

3. Place the carrots and parsnip into a saucepan, and cover with water. Bring to a boil.

4. Reduce the heat to low. Cover and simmer until the vegetables are tender, about 20–25 minutes.

5. Place into a food processor or blender. Purée until smooth. Add liquid if necessary.

### Thicken It Up

*Add too much liquid in the food processor, and your baby food will start to resemble water. Don't despair! Thicken it back up by adding a little leftover oatmeal or rice cereal, 1 teaspoon at a time, until your purée is the right consistency.*

# Broccoli and Cauliflower Purée

**3 Servings**

½ cup broccoli
½ cup cauliflower
2 cups water

*Broccoli and cauliflower are loaded with nutrients, and aren't always available in store-bought baby foods. They are both relatively strong-tasting, so if your baby doesn't like the taste of this dish, wait a few weeks and offer it again.*

•  •  •  •  •

1. Wash the broccoli. Remove the stems and leaves, and chop the florets into small pieces.

2. Wash the cauliflower. Cut the florets into small pieces, discarding the rest.

3. Place both vegetables into a steamer basket. Add water to the bottom of steamer basket. Bring to a boil and steam until tender, about 15 minutes.

4. Place into a food processor or blender. Purée for about 30 seconds.

5. Add leftover cooking water, 1 tablespoon at a time. Continue puréeing until completely smooth.

### Baby Broccoli

*For any recipe that involves broccoli, it's always possible to substitute with broccolini, or "baby broccoli." This variant is often more expensive than regular broccoli, but it is generally sweeter with a milder taste. Try puréeing it with and without the stems, and see which version your baby prefers.*

**4 Servings**

½ sweet potato
¼ small butternut squash
3 cups water

# Sweet Potato and Butternut Squash Purée

*Squashes can be quite large, so choose your vegetables with care! For this dish, you should have approximately the same amount of squash and sweet potato. If you choose a very large squash, for example, you may only need ⅛ to equal the amount of the potato.*

•   •   •   •   •

1. Wash the sweet potato and poke several holes in it with a fork. Place it directly on the oven rack or in a shallow baking pan. Bake at 400°F for 40 minutes.

2. Remove the seeds from the squash. Place face-down in a shallow pan of water. Bake alongside potato for 40 minutes.

3. Scoop the potato from the skin and place into a food processor.

4. Remove the tender meat of the squash. Combine with the potato in the food processor.

5. Purée until smooth, adding liquid as needed to achieve the desired consistency.

### Dress Up the Leftovers

*If you happen to make this recipe around Thanksgiving, try using the leftovers in the spirit of the season. Use this mixture in a custard or pie filling. Alternatively, try topping it with cinnamon sugar, and bake in the oven for a few minutes to make a fantastic side dish. Leftover squash peels can also be hollowed out and used as "boats" for meat and potato dishes.*

# Puréed Succotash

**3 Servings**

½ cup lima beans (fresh or frozen)
½ cup fresh, frozen or canned corn
2 cups water

*Most babies love corn for its sweet flavor. The hulls of the kernels, though, make corn one of the chunkier purées. Even if you add plenty of liquid and thin it as much as possible, corn purées will still have a grainier texture than sweet potatoes or carrots. If your baby gags or doesn't seem to like the texture of this dish, try again in a few weeks.*

●   ●   ●   ●   ●

1.  Put the lima beans and corn into a saucepan. If using fresh corn, remove the husk and cut the kernels from cob with a sharp knife.

2.  Cover with water; bring to a boil. Simmer until tender, about 15 minutes.

3.  Put the beans and corn into a blender or food processor. Purée for 30 seconds.

4.  Thin with the leftover cooking water, 1 tablespoon at a time. Continue puréeing until smooth.

5.  For a creamier purée, thin with breastmilk or formula instead of water.

# Sweet Potato and Avocado Purée

**3 Servings**

½ sweet potato
2 cups water
¼ avocado
3 tablespoons water,
    breastmilk, or formula

*Sweet potatoes are one of the most nutrient-dense vegetables around. Mix with avocados, and you've got one terrific healthy meal for your baby. Leftover avocado will likely oxidize and turn brown in the refrigerator, but you can sprinkle a bit of lemon juice over it to slow the process. Scoop off the lemony part before feeding, and use the remaining avocado within 1–2 days.*

●　●　●　●　●

1. Cut the sweet potato into small pieces. Cover with water in a pot, and boil until the potato is very tender.

2. Fork-mash the avocado until smooth.

3. After the potato cools, mix with the avocado and fork-mash together.

4. Add water or formula, 1 tablespoon at a time. Continue mashing until the mixture is smooth.

### Sweet Options

*Sweet potatoes can be safely cooked in a variety of ways. If you're planning to serve the leftovers at a meal for the rest of your family, consider baking the potatoes in the oven so that the skins take on a nice, crispy texture. Steaming in a shallow pan of water is also fine. After cooking, insert a knife into the potato. If the potato falls off the knife, it's done.*

# Puréed Leafy Greens

**4 Servings**

½ pound spinach or other
   leafy green
2 cups water
3 tablespoons water,
   breastmilk, or formula

*This recipe can also be made using kale, collard greens, bok choy, escarole, or almost any other type of leafy green vegetable (but remember that leafy greens, especially spinach and collard greens, have nitrates). The trick to cooking leafy greens is to remove them from the boiling water as soon as they turn bright green. Overcook, and you risk losing valuable nutrients.*

●  ●  ●  ●  ●

1. Wash the green leaves thoroughly, removing any damaged parts.

2. Steam in water for about 10 minutes, or until the vegetables turn a bright green color.

3. Allow greens to cool, then place into a food processor or blender. Purée for about 30 seconds.

4. Add water or formula, 1 tablespoon at a time. Continue puréeing until the mixture is smooth.

### Creamed Spinach
*A good variation on this dish, more suitable for older children, is creamed spinach. Heat 1 cup of milk or heavy cream with 4 tablespoons butter. Once thoroughly blended, bring the mixture to a boil. Add in about a pound of fresh spinach and continue cooking for about 5 minutes. Add sugar, nutmeg, salt, and pepper to taste.*

*½ cup dry soybeans*
*2 cups water*
*3 tablespoons water,*
    *breastmilk, or formula*

# Soybean Purée

*If your baby has ever had a problem digesting soy formula, speak to your pediatrician, who may discover an allergy or may instruct you to steer clear of this and other soy-based recipes until your child is at least 1 year old. Many soybean allergies are overcome as your child grows.*

* * * * *

1. Rinse the soybeans several times in cold water. Place into a pot, cover with water, and soak overnight in the refrigerator.

2. In the morning, drain the pot. Add 2 cups of water, bring to a boil, and then simmer for 2–2½ hours.

3. Once the beans are tender, drain and pour into a food processor or blender. Purée for 30 seconds.

4. Add water or milk, 1 tablespoon at a time. Continue puréeing until the mixture is smooth.

**Use Your Strainer**
*Even after puréeing your baby's meal until it seems thin enough, it still may be too thick or chunky for a baby to handle. If your baby gags or refuses to eat, try pouring the puréed food into a sieve or strainer. Use a rubber spatula to press the food through, and the resulting purée should be considerably thinner.*

# Red Lentil Purée

*Just about any kind of lentil can be used in this recipe. Red lentils are especially nice, though, because they cook more quickly than most other beans. Also, they generally do not need to be pre-soaked, which makes this a quick-and-easy recipe. A spiced variation of this dish, dhal, is an Indian favorite.*

●  ●  ●  ●  ●

1.  Wash and drain the lentils several times. Soak overnight if the package directions indicate that this is necessary.

2.  Sautée the onion in oil for 4–6 minutes. Add the carrot and continue cooking for another 4–5 minutes.

3.  Add the drained lentils and water. Bring to a boil, then simmer for 40–50 minutes, or until lentils are soft.

4.  Drain mixture and place into a food processor or blender, reserving the cooking liquid. Purée until smooth, adding leftover liquid 1 tablespoon at a time until the mixture is smooth.

### Beans, the Other Protein
*Chickpeas, lentils, navy beans, split peas, and other kinds of beans provide much-needed protein to an older baby's diet. Canned beans are fine to use for making baby food, as long as they are unspiced and unsalted. They generally don't need to be re-cooked. You can rinse, drain, and use them for purées straightaway.*

### 3 Servings
½ cup red lentils
1 tablespoon onion, diced
1 tablespoon oil
1 tablespoon carrot, finely chopped
2 cups water

**4 Servings**

*1 apple*
*1 carrot*
*5 tablespoons apple juice*

# Carrot-Apple Purée

*Walk through your supermarket baby food aisle, and you'll find that just about any meat, vegetable, starch, or fruit is made into a purée with apples—there's a good reason for that! Apples have a sweet, mild flavor that goes well with just about anything.*

* * * * *

1. Wash, peel, and core the apple. Cut into small chunks.

2. Wash and peel the carrot. Cut into small pieces and steam for about 15 minutes, or until tender.

3. Combine apple and carrot in a food processor or blender. Purée for about 30 seconds.

4. Add apple juice, 1 tablespoon at a time. Continue puréeing until the mixture is smooth.

**3 Servings**

*½ cup canned chickpeas*
*3 tablespoons water or
chicken stock*

# Puréed Chickpeas

*Canned chickpeas make this a very quick recipe. There's no advantage to using dried chickpeas for this dish—just be sure to use canned chickpeas with no salt added.*

* * * * *

1. Rinse and drain the chickpeas. Remove any stray hulls.

2. Place into food processor or blender, and purée for 30 seconds.

3. Add water or stock, 1 tablespoon at a time. Continue puréeing until the mixture is smooth.

# Puréed Pumpkin

**6 Servings**

½ small eating pumpkin
2 cups water

*As opposed to canned chickpeas, pumpkin is one of those foods that you want to make fresh. The color will be brighter, and the flavors will be much more vibrant.*

● ● ● ● ●

1. Remove the seeds, and cut the pumpkin off the shell. Cut into small cubes.

2. Place pumpkin cubes into a baking dish with a small amount of water. Bake at 350°F for 1 hour, or until tender.

3. Let cool, and then place pumpkin into food processor or blender, and purée until smooth. Add liquid if needed.

## Strainers and Cheesecloth
*Baby food can be strained in any number of ways. A colander or wire strainer is a good choice, and can be easily sanitized for future use. Cheesecloth can also be used for straining, especially if you're making soup or something with a lot of thick liquid. To sterilize cheesecloth after use, you'll need to boil it for 20 minutes.*

**4 Servings**

1 small ripe papaya
3 cups water

# Puréed Papaya

*Both sweet and healthy, papaya is a great food for your baby. It's full of vitamin C, folate, and potassium, and can generally be found year-round. The amount of resulting baby food depends on the size of the papaya you choose. Use a large one, and your entire family will be eating papaya for a week! Freeze the extra purée the same day you make it.*

●　●　●　●　●

1. Slice papaya in half and remove seeds. Cut into small chunks.

2. Place in a steamer basket over water, and steam for about 10 minutes, or until very tender.

3. Once cool, scrape the papaya from the skin and place into a food processor or blender.

4. Purée for about 30 seconds. Add leftover cooking water, 1 tablespoon at a time, and continue puréeing until papaya is smooth.

5. Very ripe papayas can be fork-mashed instead of puréed.

# Mashed Mango

**3 Servings**

*½ ripe mango*

*Mango is a flexible fruit that goes well with several other baby food recipes. Consider serving this with Puréed Brown Rice (page 86) or Puréed Cauliflower (page 31). Mango also freezes very well, so you can triple or quadruple this recipe to have enough for several weeks.*

* * * * *

1. Wash and peel the mango. Cut fruit away from pit and chop into pieces.

2. If the mango is not completely ripe, place in a steamer basket and steam for 15–20 minutes, or until very tender. If the mango is very ripe, you may be able to fork-mash it without cooking.

3. Allow mango to cool, then fork-mash to desired consistency.

### The Origin of Mangoes
*Mangoes are often considered to be a tropical fruit, but they're actually indigenous to Southeast Asia. They do grow best in tropical climates, and the trees can reach 50–60 feet tall. The majority of the mangoes sold in the United States originate from Mexico, South America, and the Caribbean.*

**3 Servings**

1 ripe avocado
1 ripe kiwi fruit

# Avocado and Kiwi Mash

*Kiwi fruit is a great way to get vitamins C and E into your baby's diet. You can tell a kiwi's ripe when it's plump and soft, but not overly mushy. Kiwi sweetens a bit after a while, so if your first kiwi seems too sour for your baby, let another one ripen an extra day or two before serving.*

· · · · ·

1. Cut a slice of avocado about 1 inch thick. Scoop fruit from skin.

2. Cut the kiwi in half and set aside half for a later meal. Using a spoon, scoop the fruit out of the shell. Cut off the central core and seeds, if desired (though these can be eaten). Put on a plate with the avocado.

3. Mash together with a fork until smooth. If needed, add a little breast-milk or formula for a creamier texture

4. If the mixture is not smooth enough for your baby, purée in a food processor or blender until completely puréed.

### Instead of Avocado
*Kiwi goes well with many fruits. Try cooking a peeled, cored apple for about 10 minutes, then puréeing with a peeled, seeded kiwi. For babies who like textures, fork-mash a banana and kiwi together, adding breastmilk or formula to make a creamy, fruity meal.*

# Blueberry Applesauce

**3 Servings**

*1 medium apple*
*½ cup fresh or frozen*
*blueberries*

*If fresh blueberries aren't in season, you can easily substitute frozen blueberries in this recipe. Frozen blueberries that are sold commercially are washed before freezing, so you won't need to rinse them before cooking. Only take out as many as you plan to use for cooking; return the rest to the freezer before they have time to thaw.*

• • • • •

1. Peel and core the apple, removing all seeds and skin. Cut into pieces and put into a saucepan.

2. Wash blueberries and place into the saucepan with the apple. Cover with water and bring to a boil.

3. Simmer for about 25 minutes, or until the apple and berries are completely tender.

4. Put fruit into a food processor or blender. Purée until mixture is smooth, adding water, breastmilk, or formula as necessary.

5. Pour the purée through a cheesecloth or fine strainer to remove any of the blueberry crowns.

## Strained Berries
*When cooking baby foods with berries, the meal will need to be strained before serving. Babies under a year shouldn't eat the small seeds from berries, because the seeds may be a choking hazard. A mesh strainer will do most of the work for you, but be sure the mesh is tight enough to catch the seeds.*

# Berry and Banana Mash

**1 Serving**

*5 medium blueberries*
*2 cups water*
*1 very ripe banana*

*From about 8 months on, your baby will be ready for mashed blueberry skin. If she gags or has trouble with it, push the mixture through a strainer before serving.*

· · · · ·

1. Put the berries in a pot with about 2 cups of water. Bring to a boil and simmer on the stove for about 15 minutes, or until very tender.

2. Slice off and peel about 1 inch of the banana, removing any strings.

3. Let the berries cool; then fork-mash with the banana.

# Cantaloupe Purée

**1 Serving**

*1 slice of ripe cantaloupe*

*Raw melon can be safely given to your baby from about 8 months on, but there's also no harm in steaming it first. Steaming in a basket is preferable to boiling the fruit, and will leave most of the nutritional value intact. Cantaloupe is high in vitamin A, potassium, and calcium.*

· · · · ·

1. Remove the rind from the cantaloupe. Cut into small pieces.

2. Place in a steamer basket and steam until very tender, about 8–10 minutes.

3. Place in a food processor or blender. Purée for about 30 seconds.

4. Add leftover cooking water, 1 tablespoon at a time, and continue puréeing until cantaloupe is smooth.

# Apple and Raspberry Purée

**4 Servings**

*1 medium apple*
*½ cup raspberries*

*Applesauces and purées are great foods to make in bulk. They will last for several days in the refrigerator, and the rest of the family will enjoy them as well. Use the leftover applesauce as a condiment, breakfast, or dessert. Consider taking the older children apple picking at a nearby farm, and make a day out of the harvesting!*

•  •  •  •  •

1. Peel and core the apple, removing all seeds and skin. Cut into pieces and put into a saucepan.

2. Wash raspberries and place into the saucepan with the apple. Cover with water and bring to a boil.

3. Cover and simmer for about 30 minutes, or until the apples are completely cooked.

4. Put the fruit into a food processor or blender. Purée until the mixture is smooth, adding water, breastmilk, or formula as necessary.

5. Pour the purée through a cheesecloth or fine strainer to remove any seeds from the raspberries.

## So Many Berries!

*One good substitution in this recipe, if you can't find raspberries, is to use blackberries instead. Both are members of the Rosaceae family, and they'll add the same type of flavor when mixed with apples. Blackberries are about twice as large as raspberries, though, so be sure to use only half the amount.*

**4 Servings**

*1 medium apple*
*½ fresh pear*
*¼ cup raspberries*

# Raspberry-Pear Sauce

*In addition to apples, pears also make a sweet, smooth sauce when peeled and cooked. By mixing them with apples and raspberries, you can combine three of summer's sweetest fruits in one delicious dish!*

◦　◦　◦　◦　◦

1. Peel and core the apple, removing all seeds and skin. Cut into pieces and put into a saucepan.

2. Peel and core the pear. Cut into slices and add to the saucepan.

3. Wash raspberries and place into the saucepan along with the pear and apple. Cover with water and bring to a boil.

4. Simmer for about 25 minutes, or until the apple and pear are completely tender.

5. Put fruit into a food processor or blender. Purée until mixture is smooth, adding water, breastmilk, or formula as necessary.

6. Pour the purée through a cheesecloth or fine strainer to remove any seeds.

# Berry and Pear Mash

**3 Servings**

*1 very ripe pear*
*½ cup blueberries*

*For recipes with very soft fruits, like bananas or pears, a fork is usually sufficient for mashing. If you need a smoother consistency, try using a wire potato masher instead.*

• • • • •

1. Remove skin and core from pear. Cut into small pieces.

2. Put the berries into a pot with about 2 cups of water. Bring to a boil; then simmer on the stove for about 15 minutes, or until very tender.

3. Let the berries cool; then fork-mash with the pear.

### Berry Pie

*If you end up with lot of leftover pears and berries, use them to make a pie filling for the rest of the family. Cook the pear and berries together with sugar, cinnamon, and nutmeg. Pour into a prepared pie crust, and bake at 350°F for 45–50 minutes. If your baby's teething, he might like a nibble of the pie crust too.*

**3 Servings**

¼ cup fresh dates
1 medium apple

# Apple Date Purée

*Even fresh dates are sometimes dry and hard when you buy them from a store or farmer's market. To purée successfully, they'll need to be soft and plump. The amount of time you need to soak your dates depends on what they were like when you bought them. If they're already soft, soak for 1–2 hours. If they're completely dry and hard, soak overnight in the refrigerator.*

●　●　●　●　●

1. Remove the pits from the dates. Cover with water in a dish, and allow to soak for 3–4 hours, or until they are completely hydrated.

2. Peel and core the apple. Cut into pieces and put into a saucepan.

3. Cover the apple with water; then bring to a boil. Simmer for 25 minutes, or under completely tender.

4. Drain the apple pieces and combine with soaked dates in a food processor or blender. Purée until mixture is smooth, adding water, breastmilk, or formula as necessary.

**Easy on the Dates**
*Dates are a great food because they are high in both iron and potassium. They're also high in calories, which is a good thing when you're 8 months old! They also can have a laxative effect, so try your baby out on a small amount first. If she develops loose stools, either avoid this recipe or use half the amount of dates in the recipe.*

part **4**

# 9–12 Months

**1 Serving**

2 asparagus stalks
2 cups water

# Steamed Asparagus

*When serving steamed asparagus to grownups, serve it while it's bright green by steaming it for about 5 minutes, and then plunging into ice water to stop the cooking process. Babies will need their veggies to be much more tender, though, so double the steaming time and skip the ice-water bath.*

* * * * *

1. Wash asparagus and break off ends. Cut asparagus into 2-inch-long spears. Place in steamer basket over water.

2. Bring to a boil, then steam for about 10 minutes, or until tender.

3. Allow to cool completely; then serve. Keep a close eye on the feeding session to make sure your baby doesn't choke.

**3 Servings**

½ medium zucchini
2 cups water

# Steamed Zucchini

*Summer is a great time to introduce your baby to new vegetables, especially zucchini! Soft, tender, and tasty, this vegetable can be found in abundance at local markets. It's easy to grow, too—try planting some in your garden next summer.*

* * * * *

1. Wash the zucchini thoroughly. Trim off the ends; then cut the zucchini into ¼-inch slices.

2. Place in a steamer basket inside a medium saucepan. Fill the pot with water until it reaches the bottom of the steamer basket.

3. Bring to a boil; then steam for 10–15 minutes, or until tender.

4. Cut each slice into quarters, and serve as finger food.

# Baked Winter Squash

**2 Servings**

¼ medium winter squash
2 cups water

*While most finger foods for baby are steamed rather than baked, winter squash is an exception. These hard-shelled members of the gourd family can be steamed or baked. Since winter squash are usually large, consider what to do with leftovers. Many older children will prefer baked squash (which can be topped with sugar and cinnamon) to the steamed variety, which will be milder in flavor.*

* * * * *

1. Wash the squash thoroughly. Cut it open and scoop out the seeds.

2. Place face-down in a shallow pan of water. Bake at 400°F for 45 minutes, or until squash is tender, but still slightly firm.

3. Remove from oven and allow to cool completely.

4. Cut small cubes of squash from the shell, and serve to baby as finger food.

### Winter Squash Versus Summer Squash

*Winter squash make a great finger food. They're denser than summer squash like zucchini, and hold up better when grabbed by little hands. Texture-wise, they're more similar to a carrot than a melon, and babies with a few teeth will probably handle winter squash better than their toothless friends.*

½ medium summer
squash (such as yellow
crookneck, pattipan, or
others)
2 cups water

# Steamed Summer Squash

*Summer squash are usually softer and moister than their cousin, the
winter squash. Because of this extra moisture, summer squash can be
cooked in a variety of ways. Steaming in a shallow pan of water is one
of the best, because you can retain that moisture. The leftover cooking
water can then be used if you're puréeing the squash.*

1. Wash the squash thoroughly. Cut off ends, and cut into ½-inch chunks.

2. Place into a saucepan with a small amount of water. Steam until tender,
about 10 minutes.

3. Drain the squash pieces and place in a food processor or blender.
Purée until mixture is smooth, adding water, breastmilk, or formula as
necessary. Or serve as a finger food.

**Look Ma, I Ate the Whole Thing!**
*Summer squash is similar to zucchini because the entire vegetable is
edible. Choose a squash with few surface blemishes, scrub it well
with a vegetable brush, and you can feed the entire vegetable to
babies about 8 months and older. If the squash doesn't purée
smoothly enough for your baby, use a vegetable peeler to remove the
soft skin next time.*

# Steamed Peas

*Peas are a great finger food, but watch your baby carefully to make sure she can move them around in her mouth. When in doubt, mash with a fork before serving.*

* * * * *

1. Place washed peas in a steamer basket. Put basket in a saucepan with about 2 inches of water.

2. Bring to a boil; then steam for about 10 minutes or until peas are tender.

3. Let peas cool before serving.

**1 Serving**

*½ cup fresh or frozen peas
1 cup water*

# Steamed Carrots

*When introducing finger foods, start off small. Begin with tiny pieces, about ¼-inch squares, and let your baby pick them up himself. He'll be less likely to choke if he self-feeds.*

* * * * *

1. Wash and peel carrot. Cut off the ends; then slice into 1-inch chunks.

2. Place carrot pieces in a steamer basket. Put basket in a saucepan with about 2 inches of water. Steam for 15–20 minutes, or until completely tender.

3. Let cool; then cut the carrot coins into quarters before serving.

**2 Servings**

*1 medium carrot
1 cup water*

**3 Servings**

*15 green beans*
*2 cups water*

# Steamed Green Beans

*Fresh green beans are a wonderful summer food. They're available from early summer through early fall. Frozen green beans are another good option. Canned green beans tend to be mushy and flavorless—go for fresh or frozen instead.*

* * * * *

1. Wash the beans thoroughly. Trim the ends off, removing the strings.

2. Place in a steamer basket inside a medium saucepan. Fill the pot with water until it reaches the bottom of the steamer basket.

3. Bring to a boil; then steam for 10–15 minutes, or until tender.

4. Cut each bean into quarters, and serve as finger food.

### Green Bean Side Dishes
*When beans are in season, buy and prepare them in bulk. Steam up a couple of pounds at a time. Reserve some for your baby, and try serving the rest with slivered almonds. You could also make a cold green bean salad by sautéing with garlic, olive oil, and red peppers. Green bean casserole is another family favorite.*

# Steamed Apples

**4 Servings**

1 medium apple
½ cup water

*Most steamed fruits will keep in the refrigerator for about 1 day. You can easily make 2–3 servings for immediate use, but if you plan to make a larger batch, freeze the rest. Cut into pieces and place in small freezer-safe plastic containers. Once thawed, the fruits will be ready to go.*

●　●　●　●　●

1. Wash the apple. Peel and core it; then cut into thin slices.

2. Place in a saucepan with a small amount of water. Steam until tender, about 10 minutes.

3. Drain the apple pieces and serve as finger food.

### First Finger Foods

*Once your baby is about 9 months old, it's the perfect time to introduce more finger foods. Some babies have a tendency to shove everything into their mouths at once, so be extremely vigilant while your little ones eat. Soft vegetables should be cut into pieces small enough to be picked up, but not large enough to cause choking.*

1 medium pear
½ cup water

# Steamed Pears

*Pears go well with yogurt and ice cream, so you can always turn this simple dish into a fun dessert. Place a few steamed pears in the bottom of a dish and top with a small scoop of ice cream or spoonful of vanilla yogurt.*

•   •   •   •   •

1. Wash the pear. Peel and core it; then cut into thin slices.

2. Place in a saucepan with a small amount of water. Steam until tender, about 10 minutes.

3. Drain the pear slices and serve as finger food.

### Slippery Food
*If tender apples and pears slip right through your baby's fingers, crush a bowlful of oat-ring cereal (like Cheerios) into powder, and lightly dust her fruits and vegetables with it before serving. Baby's fingers will adhere better to the fruit, so more of it makes it into her tummy.*

# Slow Cooker Applesauce

**10 Servings**

5–6 medium apples
1 teaspoon cinnamon
¼ cup sugar, optional
1 teaspoon lemon juice
½ cup water

*Slow cookers are a venerable gift to busy parents. Prepare your ingredients the night before, throw it all in the slow cooker, and have a delicious meal waiting for you at dinnertime.*

• • • • •

1. Wash, peel, and core the apples. Cut into chunks.

2. Combine all ingredients in the slow cooker. Set on low.

3. Cook for about 8 hours, stirring every hour or so, until the apples are completely cooked.

4. If the applesauce is still chunkier than you'd like, run it through a food processor or blender.

### Apple Replacements

*No apples to be found? You can make slow cooker fruit sauce from just about anything that's in season—pears, peaches, plums, etc. Just adjust the cooking time as necessary; ripe pears, for example, won't take as long to cook as firm apples.*

## Steamed Plums

**2 Servings**

1 ripe plum
1 cup water

*There is a wide variety of plums available in the summer months. Choose from many of the European varieties grown in the United States, which can range in color from green to red to purplish-blue.*

•  •  •  •  •

1.  Wash the plum. Peel and remove the pit; then cut into thin slices.

2.  If the plum is already ripe and very soft to the touch, you're done!

3.  If the plum still feels firm, place in a steamer basket in a saucepan. Add enough water so that it fills the pot under the steamer basket.

4.  Bring to a boil and then steam until tender, about 5–8 minutes.

5.  Let the plum slices cool, and then serve as finger food.

## Mashed String Beans and Pears

**3 Servings**

1 medium pear
½ cup green beans
2 cups water

*If using fresh green or yellow snap beans, choose ones that are in their prime. Extra-large older beans will be on the tough side and will be hard to mash smoothly enough. Wilted beans won't have the same fresh taste as their crisper brethren, and beans with blemishes or bad spots should also be avoided.*

•  •  •  •  •

1.  Wash, peel, and core the pear. Cut into chunks and place in a steamer basket.

2.  Wash the beans thoroughly. Trim off the ends, remove the strings, and place in the steamer basket.

3.  Add enough water so that it fills the pot under the steamer basket. Bring to a boil and steam for 10–15 minutes, or until beans are very soft. If the pears cook more quickly, remove them with a slotted spoon.

4.  Place the beans and pears on a plate, and fork-mash them together.

# Mashed Apricots and Pears

**3 Servings**

*1 medium pear
2 ripe apricots
2 cups water*

*Fork-mashing is a great technique because you can easily purée your child's food to whatever consistency you want. There's also no food processor to clean out! You should only fork-mash food that's already been steamed or food that doesn't require steaming. Mashing is not a substitute for cooking, and most food for young babies should be cooked before serving.*

•　•　•　•　•

1. Wash, peel, and core the pear. Cut into chunks and place in a steamer basket.

2. Wash, halve, and remove the pit from the apricots. Place along with pear chunks in a steamer basket.

3. Add enough water so that it fills the pot under the steamer basket. Bring to a boil and steam for 10 minutes, or until apricots are very soft.

4. Remove skins from apricots by scooping the fruit out with a spoon. Place on a plate along with the pear, and fork-mash fruit together.

### How to Skin a 'cot

*Apricots are fairly difficult to peel because their tender fruit is likely to peel off along with the skin! A good technique is to steam the apricot first; then slide a fork or spoon along the inner edge of the peel to remove the fruit. This technique also works on peaches, tomatoes, and other juicy fruits.*

**4 Servings**

1 medium pear
2 cups fresh spinach
2 cups water

# Mashed Pears and Spinach

*Spinach is definitely a powerhouse food. If your baby balks, tell her the story of Popeye, the cartoon sailor from 1929 who was able to do the work of twelve men because he ate his spinach. Your rendition of a sailor dance might also help convince her of the merits of eating spinach!*

• • • • •

1. Wash, peel, and core the pear. Cut into chunks and place in a steamer basket; then place the basket inside a saucepan.

2. Add water to fill the bottom of the saucepan. Bring to a boil and steam until pear is very tender, about 8–10 minutes.

3. If using fresh spinach, wash the leaves thoroughly, remove all stems and chop. Boil in a pan of shallow water for about 10 minutes.

4. If using frozen spinach, defrost and cook according to the package directions. You'll need about ½ cup cooked spinach for this recipe.

5. Place the spinach and pears on a plate along with the pear, and fork-mash them together. Add leftover cooking water from the pear if the mixture is too thick.

# Mashed Peaches and Sweet Potatoes

**3 Servings**

*½ small sweet potato
1 medium ripe peach*

*Peaches and sweet potatoes make for a very colorful meal. Many babies like the bright colors in this recipe and may want to feed themselves. If so, try using a bowl with a suction cup on the bottom so that it won't slide off your baby's high chair tray, and give him a rubber- or plastic-coated spoon so he won't hurt his gums.*

•  •  •  •  •

1.  Scrub the sweet potato and poke several holes in it. Bake at 400°F for 40 minutes.

2.  Wash the peach and cut in half. Remove the pit and any of the harder inner fruit.

3.  Scoop the peach out of the peel, or remove the peel with a paring knife. Place on a large plate.

4.  When the sweet potato is cool, scoop the potato out of the peel. Combine on plate with peach, and fork-mash together.

5.  Mashing the peach may release more juice that you need, causing the meal to become too runny. Drain off the juice as required, and continue mashing until the mixture has a fairly smooth consistency.

**4 Servings**

1 medium carrot
1 small white potato
½ cup cooked chicken
2 cups water

# Puréed Vegetables with Chicken

*This is a great meal to make from leftovers. Making roast chicken with carrots and potatoes for supper? Mash it up for your baby! Feed it to her at the table, along with the rest of the family, so you create family mealtime traditions.*

●　●　●　●　●

1. Wash and peel the carrot. Cut into coin-sized dices and place in a saucepan. Wash and peel the potato. Cut into small cubes and add to the saucepan.

2. Add enough water to cover the vegetables. Bring to a boil; then cook for 15–20 minutes or until the vegetables are very tender.

3. Remove all fat, skin, and bones from chicken. Dice.

4. Remove vegetables and place on plate along with chicken. Fork-mash until it reaches a consistency suitable for your baby. Or purée in a food processor or food mill to produce a smoother texture.

5. Add breastmilk or formula, 1 teaspoon at a time, to make the mixture smoother.

**Scrape It Down**
*If you're using a full-sized food processor to purée ¼ cup vegetables and meat, don't be surprised if your ingredients all stick to the sides of the processor bowl. Stop the processor every few seconds to scrape down the sides, pushing all the food back into the blades.*

# Puréed Turkey and Cranberries

*Just about any kind of cranberries can be used for this recipe. If you don't want to use fresh ones, the canned varieties are fine—jellied cranberries won't even need cooking or puréeing before serving. If using canned whole-berry cranberries, run the berries through a blender or food processor before serving.*

•   •   •   •   •

**4 Servings**

½ cup cooked turkey
½ cup fresh cranberries
1 tablespoon sugar
¼ cup water

1. Mix the water and sugar in a saucepan. Bring to a boil and cook at a high temperature for 2–3 minutes, stirring constantly.

2. Add cranberries. Reduce heat to a simmer; then cook for 15–20 minutes. Cranberries should burst, and the mixture will thicken.

3. Allow cranberries to cool completely.

4. Dice turkey. Mix with cranberries and fork-mash together until they reach a consistency your baby will accept. You can also purée the mixture in a food processor or food mill.

5. Add breastmilk or formula, 1 teaspoon at a time, to make the mixture smoother.

**3 Servings**

¼ cup thin pasta
1 cup fresh or frozen
   spinach
2 cups water

# Puréed Spinach with Pasta

*While pasta noodles make a great finger food, they're really more
suitable in their whole form for older babies (or babies with a few
teeth). You cantry fork-mashing this dish for a "Step 3" type of meal,
but may have more success with the food processor.*

•   •   •   •   •

1. Place pasta in a pot and cover with water. Boil for 20–25 minutes, or
   until pasta is very tender.

2. If using fresh spinach, wash the leaves thoroughly, remove stems, and
   chop. Boil in a pan of shallow water for 10 minutes. If using frozen spinach, defrost and cook according to the package directions.

3. Combine the cooked spinach and pasta in a food processor or blender.
   Purée for about 30 seconds.

4. Add breastmilk or formula, 1 tablespoon at a time. Continue puréeing
   until the mixture reaches a creamy consistency.

**Pasta Differences**

*For the purpose of puréed baby food, try to use a pasta that cooks up
soft, such as tubular or ribbon noodles. Like your spaghetti al dente?
Overcook it for baby, since chewy or hard noodles will not purée well.
Also avoid whole-wheat pastas—they may be healthier, but usually
have a firmer consistency.*

# Chicken and Broccoli

*Leftover roast chicken is a versatile ingredient for all sorts of simple dinners for your baby. Here, it's paired with tasty and nutritious broccoli, which also mashes to a smooth consistency when well-cooked.*

● ● ● ● ●

**4 Servings**

*1 broccoli crown*
*½ cup cooked chicken*
*1 cup water*

1. Wash the broccoli. Peel the stem with vegetable peeler, or discard the stem. Cut into small pieces and place in a steamer basket in a small saucepan.

2. Add enough water to reach the bottom of the steamer basket. Bring to a boil; then cook for 15 minutes or until the broccoli is very tender.

3. Remove all fat, skin, and bones from chicken. Dice.

4. Remove broccoli from steamer and place on plate along with chicken. Fork-mash until it reaches a consistency suitable for your baby.

5. Add breastmilk or formula, 1 tablespoon at a time, to make the mixture smoother.

**4 Servings**

1 small sweet potato
1 small boneless, skinless
    chicken breast (about
    6 ounces)

# Chicken and Sweet Potatoes

*If you're all out of sweet potatoes, try using butternut or acorn
squash instead. Squash tends to be more watery than potato, so
you may need less liquid while puréeing.*

•   •   •   •   •

1. Wash the sweet potato, remove the skin and cut into cubes. Place in a
   pot and cover with water.

2. Bring the water to a boil; then cook for about 25 minutes or until potato
   is completely tender. Save the cooking liquid.

3. Place the chicken in a separate small saucepan, and cover with water.
   Bring to a boil and cook for about 20 minutes, or until the internal temperature reaches 170°F.

4. After both chicken and potato have cooled, combine in a food processor or blender. Pulse for 30 seconds.

5. Add breastmilk or formula, 1 tablespoon at a time, to make the mixture
   smoother. Continue puréeing until smooth.

### Pasty Purée

*Are your chicken-based purées coming out either too chunky or too
pasty? Try adding a little bit of butter or margarine if your baby is older
than 6 months. It may smooth out the mixture just enough to please
even a fussy eater. If your child is sensitive to dairy products, try a
non-dairy margarine.*

# Chicken and Peach Mash

**4 Servings**

½ cup cooked chicken
¼ cup white or brown rice,
    cooked
½ very ripe peach

*This dinner-dessert combo is a great meal to make from leftovers. Whenever you're making chicken and rice for the rest of the family, reserve some lightly spiced (or unseasoned) leftovers for baby. You can also substitute apricots for peaches, as long as the fruit is very ripe and easy to peel.*

●　●　●　●　●

1. Slice the peach in half, removing the pit and any hard parts around the pit.

2. Using a spoon, scoop the peach flesh out of the skin. Mash with a fork; then drain the leftover juice into a small dish.

3. Dice chicken. Add to a plate with the peach.

4. Add rice. Fork-mash until the mixture is well combined.

5. Add the leftover peach juice as necessary to thin the mash. If it's still too thick, add either extra peach juice, breastmilk, or formula, one tablespoon at a time, to make the mixture smoother. Continue mashing until smooth. Alternatively, purée in food processor for a smoother consistency.

## Apricots and Peaches

*Like peaches, apricots are stone fruits that, when ripe, have a very high moisture content. That means when you're fork-mashing, expect juice to come running out. Peach recipes can generally use apricots as a substitute, but make sure to double or triple the amount of fruit, because apricots are considerably smaller than peaches.*

## 4 Servings

½ cup lean beef (about
    4 ounces)
1 medium carrot
½ small onion

# Puréed Beef and Carrots

*When fork-mashing beef for your baby, it pays to use more tender cuts of beef.
Don't go for the tough stew meat, and also be sure to cook the meat slowly, to lock
in both flavor and liquid. For babies who aren't that good at chewing or gumming
chewier foods, you may want stick to puréeing this dish in the food processor.*

•　•　•　•　•

1. Peel and slice the onion into thin pieces. Sauté in a deep non-stick pan until soft and translucent. Use butter or vegetable oil to keep onions from sticking to the pan, if necessary.

2. Add the beef to the pan, covering with water. Bring to a boil; then simmer for about 40 minutes.

3. Wash and peel the carrot, and cut into ½-inch chunks. Add to the meat pot and simmer for another 20 minutes, or until the meat is completely cooked and tender.

4. Remove the meat and carrot from the pot, and cool completely. Place in a food processor or blender and pulse for 30 seconds. Mash with fork for older babies.

5. Add water, breastmilk, or formula, 1 tablespoon at a time, to make the mixture smoother. Continue pureeing until smooth.

# Chicken, Carrots, and Rice

*Remember that meat dishes should be served to babies from about 8 months and up. These ages are somewhat flexible, depending on your baby's growth and development. Some pediatricians recommend not serving meat until 10 months, while some suggest babies as young as 6 months have their first chicken or beef.*

· · · · ·

**4 Servings**

½ cup cooked chicken
¼ cup cooked white or
    brown rice
1 medium carrot

1. Wash and peel the carrots. Cut into small pieces.

2. Place in a saucepan with enough water to cover the carrots. Bring the water to a boil; then simmer until the carrots are very tender, about 15–20 minutes.

3. Place the carrots in a food processor or blender with the rice.

4. Dice chicken. Add to the food processor, and purée for 30 seconds.

5. Add water, breastmilk, or formula, 1 tablespoon at a time, to make the mixture smoother. Continue puréeing until smooth.

**The Best Liquid**

*While water is an effective thinner, you can also use homemade chicken or vegetable stock, if your baby has already tried them. Don't use them in combination recipes until you're sure that they are well tolerated, and avoid store-bought bouillons, which contain a lot of salt and other spices.*

½ cup cooked beef
¼ small butternut squash
¼ cup cooked pasta

# Beef, Squash, and Pasta

*Don't be afraid to try new food combinations for your baby. By combining a meat, a starch, and a vegetable, you can get a complete meal in each spoonful!*

* * * * *

1.  Remove the seeds from the squash. Place face-down in a shallow pan of water. Bake for about 40 minutes at 400°F.

2.  Allow to cool; then scoop out the squash flesh and place in food processor or blender. Chop the beef into small pieces, and add to food processor. Add pasta.

3.  Purée as needed to reach desired consistency. Add water, breastmilk, or formula, 1 tablespoon at a time, to thin out the mixture.

**2 Servings**

1 small apple
½ cup cooked chicken

# Chicken and Apples

*Chicken and apples is a great combination for babies. They love the sweet apples, and you can feel good that they're getting some much-needed protein from the chicken. This healthful meal can be served either warm or cold.*

* * * * *

1.  Wash and peel the apple; then cut into small pieces.

2.  Place the apple in a saucepan and cover with water. Bring the water to a boil; then cook for about 20 minutes, or until the apple is very tender.

3.  Combine the chicken and apple on a plate. Fork-mash until tender.

4.  If the mixture is too thick, add the leftover cooking water from the apple, 1 teaspoon at a time.

# Beef, Peas, and Potatoes

*Combination dinners help include your baby in meals with the family. Just remove a small portion of the entrée and side dishes before adding extra seasonings, and purée for your baby.*

* * * * *

1. Wash, peel, and dice potato. Place in a saucepan, cover with water, and boil for 10–15 minutes.

2. Add peas to saucepan. Boil for another 5–10 minutes until peas and potatoes are both very tender.

3. Let cool; then place in food processor with beef. Purée as needed to reach desired consistency, adding leftover cooking water to thin out the mixture.

## Pasta Flours
*Pasta dough is usually made of unbleached white flour or semolina flour, but you can find it made with just about any grain: oat flour, corn flour, buckwheat flour, or even mung bean threads. If your baby has a wheat allergy, try substituting standard pasta with one made of these alternate flours.*

**3 Servings**

*½ cup cooked beef*
*½ cup peas (fresh or frozen)*
*1 small potato (or ½ large potato)*

½ cup cooked chicken
1 cup water
½ cup green beans (fresh or
  frozen)
1 medium carrot

# Chicken, Carrots, and Green Beans

*Green beans are a great source of vitamin C. Make sure to remove all the strings from them before cooking, otherwise the beans will be too fibrous to purée well and will cause your baby problems when he tries to eat them. Try to use fresh green beans in the summer, although frozen ones are a good substitute in winter months.*

* * * * *

1. Wash and peel the carrot. Cut into small pieces. Place into a saucepan with enough water to cover the carrot pieces. Bring the water to a boil; then simmer until the carrots begin to get tender, about 10 minutes.

2. While the carrots are cooking, break off the ends of the green beans (if fresh) and pull the strings off the sides. Cut into small pieces.

3. Add the green beans to the partially cooked carrots, adding more water if necessary to cover. Cook for another 10 minutes or so, until both carrots and beans are tender.

4. Place the carrots in a food processor or blender, along with the beans and chicken. Purée for 30 seconds.

5. Add water, breastmilk, or formula, 1 tablespoon at a time, to make the mixture smoother. Continue puréeing until smooth.

# Pork, Green Beans, and Potatoes

*Pork is a simple meat that can be easy for babies to eat and enjoy. If your family is having pork roast or pork chops for dinner, save a piece of the unseasoned meat to purée for your baby. Make sure to cut out any gristle or tough parts before chopping up the meat. As with all meats you serve your baby, make sure that the pork is thoroughly cooked.*

• • • • •

1. Wash and peel the potato. Cut into small pieces and place into a saucepan.

2. Break off the ends of the green beans (if fresh) and pull the strings off the sides. Cut into small pieces. Place in the saucepan with the potato pieces.

3. Add enough water to cover the potato and string bean pieces. Bring the water to a boil; then simmer until the potatoes and beans are very tender, about 15 minutes.

4. Place the beans, potatoes, and pork in a food processor or blender and purée for 30 seconds.

5. Add cooking water, breastmilk, or formula, 1 tablespoon at a time, to make the mixture smoother. Continue puréeing until smooth.

## Foods Made with Breastmilk

*Unlike mixtures made with cow's milk or formula, foods thinned with breastmilk tend to get thinner over time if they sit because the natural compounds in breastmilk, such as lipase, tend to break down the food and cause it to become thinner. This means that it's better to mix foods with breastmilk right before serving them.*

---

**4 Servings**

½ cup cooked pork, chopped
½ cup green beans (fresh or frozen)
1 cup water
1 small potato (or ½ large potato)

---

½ cup cooked turkey
½ cup corn (fresh, frozen, or
   canned)
1 small sweet potato (or half
   a large sweet potato)

# Turkey, Sweet Potatoes, and Corn

*Thanksgiving is about sharing, and babies need to be included as much as everyone else. Once your baby is starting to crave solid foods, she'll probably try swiping the turkey off your plate anyway. Dark meat tends to be more moist than white meat, so it will be easier for your baby to chew.*

* * * * *

1. If using fresh corn, remove husk and then use a knife to cut kernels from the cob.

2. Peel the sweet potato and chop into pieces. Place in the saucepan with the corn kernels.

3. Add enough water to cover the corn and sweet potatoes. Bring the water to a boil; then simmer until the vegetables are very tender, about 15 minutes.

4. Place the corn, sweet potatoes, and turkey into a food processor or blender. and purée for 30 seconds.

5. Add cooking water, breastmilk, or formula, 1 tablespoon at a time, to make the mixture smoother. Continue puréeing until smooth. This mixture will be somewhat thicker than other purées due to the corn kernels, so be sure that your baby's ready for the texture.

# Chicken Stew with Barley

*Stew is a great meal for your baby because the rest of the family can eat it as-is, just skip the puréeing step! Also, you might want to add seasonings (salt, pepper, thyme, or parsley) and cook an extra 10 minutes before serving to older children or adults.*

**5 Servings**

1 small chicken breast
(about 4 ounces)
1 small white potato
1 medium carrot
¼ cup cooked barley
1 cup water

●  ●  ●  ●  ●

1. Wash the chicken thoroughly and cut into 1-inch pieces. Place in a saucepan. Cover with water and bring to a boil, and cook for about 10 minutes.

2. Wash, peel, and slice the carrot into ½-inch chunks. Add to the cooking pot.

3. Wash, peel, and chop the potato into ½-inch cubes. Add to the cooking pot, and continue cooking until everything is completely cooked and tender, about 20–25 minutes longer.

4. Once cooled, place the stewed ingredients into a food processor, along with the cooked barley. Purée until smooth, adding breastmilk or formula as needed to thin it out.

**A Starch Is a Starch Is a Starch . . .**
*When it comes to baby food, you can generally substitute one starch for another without hearing any complaints. If you don't have any white potatoes on hand, substitute half of a sweet potato or yam. If you happen to have leftover rice from last night's dinner, use that instead.*

**5 Servings**

1 small chicken breast
(about 4 ounces)
¼ cup cooked white or
brown rice
½ cup water
¼ cup chicken stock

# Chicken Rice Dinner

*This meal is easy to prepare because both ingredients (chicken and rice) take the same amount of time to prepare, cook, and cool. Since the meal involves meat, be prepared to freeze the leftovers on the same day you make the recipe.*

●　●　●　●　●

1. Wash the chicken thoroughly and place into a saucepan.

2. Cover with water and bring to a boil. Cook for 20–25 minutes, or until chicken is thoroughly cooked.

3. Combine the rice with ½ cup water in another saucepan. Bring to a boil; then simmer for 20 minutes, or until all liquid has been absorbed.

4. Cut cooked cooled chicken into pieces and combine with rice in the food processor. Purée for 30 seconds.

5. Thin the purée with either water or chicken broth, 1 tablespoon at a time, as needed.

# Fruity Chicken Stew

*Want to make this sweet recipe even sweeter? Try thinning out the stew with apple juice or peach juice instead of water. You can even use apple cider as a liquid, as long as it's been pasteurized.*

*　•　•　•　•　•*

1. Wash the chicken thoroughly, cut into 1-inch pieces, and place in a saucepan. Cover with water and bring to a boil, and cook for about 10 minutes.

2. Wash, peel, and slice the carrot into ½-inch chunks. Add to the cooking pot.

3. Wash, peel, and chop the apple into ½-inch cubes. Add to the cooking pot, and continue cooking until everything is completely cooked and tender, about 20–25 minutes longer.

4. Wash the peach and remove the pit and skin. Dice.

5. Once cooled, place the stewed ingredients into a food processor, along with the cooked rice and diced peach. Purée until smooth, adding breastmilk or formula as needed to thin it out.

### But My Peaches Aren't Ripe!

*If peaches aren't quite in season or the ones you have aren't especially ripe, don't despair. Boiling or steaming for 10–15 minutes should soften them up enough for either puréeing or fork-mashing. Use the same trick for other stone fruits (such as apricots and plums). Remember that they won't be as sweet as naturally ripe fruit.*

**5 Servings**

1 small boneless, skinless chicken breast (about 4 ounces)
½ medium apple
½ very ripe peach
1 medium carrot
½ cup cooked rice
1 cup water

**2 Servings**

¼ cup regular oats (not
    quick-cooking)
½ very ripe banana
1 cup water

# Banana Oatmeal

*As soon as your baby's had her first oatmeal and shows no sign of aller-
gies, mix it up! Banana oatmeal is a great early cereal because it combines two of the foods that are easiest to digest: cereal and bananas.*

● ● ● ● ●

1. Grind the oats into a powder, using either a food processor or blender.
   Alternatively, a mortar and pestle makes a terrific grinder for a small
   amount.

2. Pour water into a small saucepan. Bring to a rolling boil. Add the powdered
   oats to the boiling water, stirring constantly for about 30 seconds.

3. Cover the pot, turn down the heat to low, and simmer for 8–10 minutes,
   or until the oats are smooth and thick. Stir occasionally to prevent sticking and burning.

4. Peel the banana, removing any brown spots. Fork-mash on a plate until
   completely creamed.

5. Mix the banana with the cooled cereal. Add breastmilk or formula to
   thin, if necessary.

# Pear Oatmeal

*Pears make a great addition to oatmeal. Because of their relatively high juice content, you probably won't even need to add liquid to thin the oatmeal later—just use the leftover pear juice.*

**2 Servings**

¼ cup regular oats (not quick-cooking)
½ very ripe pear
1 cup water

* * * * *

1. Grind the oats into a powder, using either a food processor or blender. Alternatively, a mortar and pestle makes a terrific grinder for a small amount.

2. Pour the water into a small saucepan. Bring to a rolling boil. Add the powdered oats to the boiling water, stirring constantly for about 30 seconds.

3. Cover the pot, turn down the heat to low, and simmer for 8–10 minutes, or until the oats are smooth and thick. Stir occasionally to prevent sticking and burning.

4. Remove the core and skin from the pear. Dice into pieces, and then fork-mash on a plate until completely smooth.

5. Mix the pear with the cooled cereal.

### Rib-Stickin' Good?

*A hearty bowl of oatmeal is supposed to stick to the ribs, right? If you feed baby oatmeal for breakfast, does that mean he'll be satisfied until lunchtime? Not on your life! Most babies will snack every couple of hours, regardless of what they've just eaten.*

**2 Servings**

¼ cup brown rice
½ cup water

# Puréed Brown Rice

*Puréed rice is a step up from Simple Rice Cereal (page 10) because the end result has more texture. This recipe is perfect for babies who prefer food they can mash around with their gums. It can be served as a cereal, or as a lunch or dinner dish.*

·　·　·　·　·

1. Combine the rice and water in a small saucepan. Bring to a roiling boil.

2. Cover the pot, turn down the heat to low and simmer for 35 minutes, or until the water is completely absorbed.

3. Allow the rice to cool, then place into food processor or blender. Pulse for 30 seconds.

4. Add breastmilk or formula, 1 tablespoon at a time, and purée until the rice is the desired consistency.

**10 Servings**

1 cup all-purpose flour
1 cup graham flour or rye flour
2 tablespoons sugar
½ teaspoon baking soda
½ teaspoon baking powder
1 cup cornmeal
3 tablespoons margarine or vegetable shortening
¾ cup milk, water, or soy milk

# Swedish Teething Cookies

*This version of Swedish hard bread, called Knackbrod, is intended to crumble slowly in your baby's mouth as she gnaws on it. The melt-in-the-mouth consistency is perfect for teething.*

·　·　·　·　·

1. Preheat oven to 350° F. Mix together all dry ingredients. Cut in margarine or shortening with two forks or pastry blender until the mixture resembles fine crumbs.

2. Add liquid and mix well.

3. Roll dough out ½ inch thick and cut into shapes (rectangles are easy for a baby to grasp, but also try circles, crescents, or other shapes if desired).

4. Bake for 10–15 minutes until hard and brown.

# Banana Apple Farina

*Farina is a good alternative to the standard oatmeal and rice cereal recipes. Because it's made of wheat, be sure not to serve to any child with a wheat allergy or sensitivity. This recipe can also be made with milk instead of water for children older than 1 year old.*

• • • • •

**4 Servings**

*3 tablespoons farina*
*½ cup unsweetened*
   *applesauce*
*½ very ripe banana*
*1 cup water*

1. Bring the water to a boil. Add farina and stir well.

2. Reduce heat and cook until the farina thickens, about 1–3 minutes, stirring continuously. Remove from the heat and allow to cool for about 10 minutes.

3. Peel banana, removing any brown spots. Fork-mash until completely creamed.

4. Stir the applesauce and banana into the cooled cereal.

### Where Do I Find Farina?
*Baby rice and baby oatmeal are common staples in the neighborhood grocery store. Farina, though, may be a little more difficult to find. Try looking in the hot-cereal aisle, next to quick-cooking oats and other breakfast cereals.*

**20 Servings**

⅔ cup milk or water
4 tablespoons butter, melted
    and cooled, or vegetable
    oil
1 tablespoon brown sugar
1 cup wheat germ (toasted
    or untoasted)
1 cup whole-wheat flour

# Homemade Biter Biscuits

*Once your baby is teething, you'll want to have a variety of hard, crispy teething biscuits or cookies on hand. The goal in making these treats is that the end product should be hard and crunchy, and not crumble or break off in big pieces in your baby's mouth.*

•   •   •   •   •

1. Beat together milk or water, butter or oil, and sugar.

2. Stir in wheat germ and flour, and knead for 8–10 minutes until dough is smooth and satiny. Add more water or more flour if necessary.

3. Make small balls of dough and roll them into sticks that are about ½-inch thick and 4 inches long.

4. Roll out on floured surface to a ½-inch thickness.

5. Bake on a greased cookie sheet at 350°F for 45 minutes, or until the biscuits are hard and browned.

### Teething Biscuit Safety
*Wait until your baby can comfortably eat solid puréed foods before offering her a teething biscuit. Always supervise your baby carefully while she's eating one—ideally she'll gnaw on the hard biscuit, getting relief for her sore gums while eating some of it, very slowly, in the process. But it's always possible that she could break off a piece big enough to choke on, so be careful.*

# Homemade Graham Crackers

*Graham flour is a coarser version of whole-wheat flour that includes more of the nutrient-rich parts of the wheat kernel. Graham flour can spoil quickly, so store it in your refrigerator and use within 2–3 months. You can also substitute regular whole-wheat flour in this recipe, but it won't have the full nutty taste of graham crackers.*

•  •  •  •  •

1. Combine flours, salt, baking powder, and sugar.

2. Cut in butter, margarine, or shortening until the dough has the consistency of cornmeal.

3. Add milk or water and knead to make a stiff dough. The dough will be very crumbly—press together. Roll out on floured surface to a ½-inch thickness.

4. Cut into squares and prick with a fork. Brush with milk or water, if desired.

5. Bake at 400°F on baking sheet for 15–20 minutes, or until golden brown. Separate squares and loosen from pan once cooked, but leave on baking sheet to cool.

**10 Servings**

*1 cup graham or whole-wheat flour*
*1 cup unbleached flour*
*1 teaspoon salt*
*1 teaspoon baking powder*
*½ cup sugar*
*¼ cup margarine, butter, or shortening*
*⅓ cup milk or water*

**10 Servings**

1 cup all-purpose flour
1 cup baby cereal (rice,
    oatmeal, etc.)
1 cup apple juice

# Baby Cereal Cookies

*Baby cereals, such as rice or oatmeal, can also be baked into these simple teething cookies. Instead of pre-made cereals, of course, you can just use your own ground-up rice or oatmeal. Be forewarned that the dough in this recipe may be very sticky!*

•   •   •   •   •

1.  Mix all ingredients well, adding more flour or baby cereal if necessary to achieve a doughlike consistency. Dough will be sticky.

2.  Roll dough out to ½-inch thick and cut into sticks, about 1-inch wide and 3-inches thick.

3.  Bake at 350°F for 20–30 minutes, or until dry and hard.

## Other Great Teething Foods

*In addition to the array of teething foods presented here, there are other great items that your child may enjoy teething on that may soothe her sore gums. One option is a frozen washcloth—simply run a clean washcloth under cold water and pop it in the freezer. No choking hazards, and  your baby will at least be momentarily amused by her cold "snack."*

# Whole-Wheat Teething Crackers

*Another simple nutritious teething cracker, this recipe is doubly good for your baby because it uses both whole-wheat flour and wheat germ. Wheat germ comes from the heart of the wheat kernel, and is a source of essential nutrients such as vitamin E, folic acid, phosphorus, zinc, thiamin, and magnesium.*

●　●　●　●　●

**10 Servings**

3 cups oatmeal
1 cup whole-wheat flour
1 cup unbleached white flour
1 cup wheat germ
3 tablespoons sugar
1 teaspoon salt, optional
¾ cup oil
1 cup water

1. Preheat oven to 350°F. Mix together oatmeal, flours, wheat germ, and sugar. Beat together oil and water, and work into dry ingredients to form a soft dough.

2. Roll dough out onto 2 cookie sheets; sprinkle with salt. Roll dough again lightly to press salt into dough.

3. Cut dough into squares with knife or pizza cutter.

4. Bake crackers for 15 minutes. Check crackers and remove those that are hard and golden brown. Continue cooking remainder, checking every 3–5 minutes to remove any that are baked. Cool on rack; then store tightly covered.

### What a Mess!

*Don't be surprised when your child gets more of a teething biscuit on his face, hands, and clothes than he does in his mouth! While different biscuits have different consistencies, the basic idea is that the hard biscuit soothes your child's gums, while dissolving slowly. Once your baby starts getting larger pieces of the biscuit off, it's time to throw away the remainder and do some cleanup.*

**12 Servings**

1 package active dry yeast
¼ cup warm water
½ cup plus 1 tablespoon
    sugar
4 cups all-purpose flour
2 egg yolks
¼ cup margarine or butter,
    melted
1 cup milk, water, or soy
    milk

# Zwieback Toast

*Why buy these popular baby toasts from the store when you
can make them yourself? Make enough for a couple days, or
prepare a larger batch to get you through the week.*

* * * * *

1. Pour the yeast, 1 tablespoon of flour, and 1 tablespoon sugar into the warm water. Mix until dissolved; then allow it to sit for 10–15 minutes, or until the yeast forms a sponge.

2. Add 2 cups of flour and 1 cup of milk to the yeast. Stir to dissolve; then let rest for 5 minutes.

3. Add the remaining ingredients, mixing thoroughly. Place in a greased bowl and allow to rise for about 2 hours, or until doubled in bulk. Punch down and knead for about 5 minutes.

4. Shape the dough into 3-inch balls. Place on a greased baking sheet and allow to rise for another 2 hours, or until doubled again.

5. Bake at 375°F for 20 minutes. Let cool, then cut into ½-inch slices. Return to the oven and bake until the slices are browned, for 20–30 minutes.

### Isn't There an Easier Way?
*A quick Zwieback toast can be made by simply taking a slice of whole-wheat bread, cutting it into ½-inch slices, and popping it into the oven. Bake at 250°F for 1 hour, or until the toasts are hard. Be sure not to cook at too high a temperature (or too near the top of the oven), or the Zwieback will burn.*

# Baby Teething Biscotti

*A baby shouldn't have egg whites until she is at least 1 year old; older babies can better digest egg white protein, and it also will lessen the chance of an egg allergy developing. Egg yolks can start to be given at 6–8 months, so be sure you're using only the yolks in these biscuit recipes.*

⚬ ⚬ ⚬ ⚬ ⚬

**8–10 Servings**

1 cup all-purpose flour
2 tablespoons brown sugar
½ teaspoon baking powder
¼ teaspoon baking soda
1 egg yolk
1 tablespoon oil
⅓ cup milk, water, or soy milk

1. Mix together flour, sugar, baking powder, and baking soda.

2. Add egg yolk, oil, and milk. Stir until the mixture forms a firm dough.

3. Shape the dough into a log about 6 inches long. Place on a greased cookie sheet, and press the log into a bar about 2 inches wide. Bake at 325°F for 20 minutes then cool until the log is cool enough to touch.

4. Cut diagonally into ½-inch slices. Spread out on the cookie sheet; then bake for another 10–15 minutes. Slices should be crispy and dry.

5. Cool on wire racks.

1 cup self-rising flour
¼ cup butter or margarine
1 egg yolk
¼ cup milk, water, or soy
    milk

# Quick Teething Rusks

*Rusks, usually called cookies in North America, are a type of hard biscuit that are great for teething because they absorb liquid. With babies, this liquid tends to be saliva! But adults can dunk rusks in milk or coffee.*

•   •   •   •   •

1. Preheat oven to 375°F. Cut the butter into the flour with a fork. Mix together until coarse crumbs are formed.

2. Add in the egg yolk and milk. Stir until it forms a smooth dough, adding more or less liquid as necessary.

3. Roll the dough to a 1-inch thickness on a lightly floured surface. Cut into 1-inch slices and place on a greased cookie sheet.

4. Bake at 375°F for 20-25 minutes, or until browned. Cool on a wire rack.

### Other Ways to Crisp a Biscuit

*Cooking baby biscuits is more of an art than a science. While it's easiest to bake them all in one go, you can shorten the cooking time by "flash cooking" at a higher temperature for the first 10–15 minutes. You'll want to lower the temperature after that, though, to avoid burning before the biscuits are thoroughly cooked.*

# Sesame Teething Crackers

*Sesame is a fun new taste for baby, and probably a pleasant change from rice and oatmeal! Any recipe with seeds should only be given to babies 8 months and older. Younger babies may have difficulty swallowing the seeds.*

• • • • •

1. Preheat oven to 350°F. Mix the flours and oil together in a bowl. Add sesame seeds and stir well.

2. Add water and continue mixing; the dough should reach a slightly sticky consistency.

3. Place dough on a lightly floured surface. Roll to about ⅛-inch thickness, and cut into 1-inch strips.

4. Bake on an ungreased cookie sheet for 20–25 minutes, or until the crackers are brown and crispy.

## 12 Servings

¾ cup all-purpose flour
¼ cup whole-wheat flour
2 tablespoons oil
2 tablespoons fresh sesame seeds
¼ cup milk, water, or soy milk
¼ teaspoon salt, optional

1 quart whole milk
⅓ cup nonfat dry milk
   powder
3 tablespoons sugar
¼ cup commercial
   unflavored, cultured
   yogurt (or ¼ cup
   homemade yogurt)

# Homemade Whole-Fat Yogurt

*Making your own whole-fat yogurt is a bit complicated, but the results are great. You'll need a small amount of commercial yogurt as a "starter," but once you start making your own yogurt, you can save a bit to start the next batch and just replenish the commercial starter every 5 batches or so.*

•   •   •   •   •

1. Select heat-safe container(s) for finished yogurt, either a 5-cup container or individual smaller containers, and fill with boiling water to keep warm. Preheat oven to 200°F and turn off. Monitor oven temperature with oven thermometer and turn on periodically to keep temperature at 108°F–112°F.

2. Place cold milk in top of double boiler. Stir in nonfat dry milk powder and sugar. Heat milk to 200°F. Measure temperature using a candy thermometer. Hold at this temperature for 10 minutes, stirring gently. Do not boil.

3. Remove the top of the double boiler and place in cold water. Monitor temperature and cool rapidly to 112°F–115°F. Remove pan from cold water once it reaches this temperature.

4. Remove 1 cup of warm milk from the pan and blend the yogurt starter culture with it. Add to rest of warm milk. Temperature should be 110°F–112°F. Pour yogurt immediately into pre-warmed container(s). Cover and place in oven. Incubate in oven for 4 hours, monitoring temperature and turning oven on and off as needed to keep between 108°F –112°F.

5. Refrigerate yogurt immediately. Yogurt will keep in refrigerator for up to 10 days. Save a small amount as the starter for your next batch of yogurt.

### Starting Dairy Products
*Once your baby is about 9 months old, she'll be ready for cultured dairy products. Yogurt is a great first dairy product to start with because the active cultures in it will help your baby digest the milk better. This is why your baby can have yogurt and cheese before she's 1 year old, but needs to wait until after 1 year before having plain cow's milk.*

# Vanilla Yogurt

*Commercial or homemade plain yogurt can be made sweeter and tastier for your baby with a few simple additions. Try your baby on plain yogurt first, but if he seems not to like the sour taste, try this sweeter version.*

• • • • •

1. Place yogurt in a bowl.

2. Stir in vanilla and sugar. Mix until smooth.

3. Use immediately, or refrigerate extra and use within 2–3 days.

**2 Servings**

*1 cup plain whole-fat yogurt, homemade or commercial*
*½ teaspoon vanilla extract*
*2 tablespoons sugar*

# Yogurt with Melon

*Cantaloupe and honeydew are mild in flavor, and mix well with yogurt. If your melons aren't ripe enough to mash easily, purée in the food processor before blending with yogurt.*

• • • • •

1. Cut a thin slice of a ripe melon, and remove all seeds. Slice the fruit off of the rind and fork-mash on a plate.

2. Blend in the yogurt with a spoon. Mix thoroughly.

**Leftover Melon**

*Most babies will not consume an entire honeydew at a week's worth of sittings, much less a single meal. For the grownups, try slicing up the leftovers and serving with a thin piece of prosciutto on top. Children like the fun shape of melon balls—use a melon-ball tool or, if your children are big eaters, an ice-cream scoop!*

**1 Serving**

*1 slice honeydew or cantaloupe*
*3 tablespoons whole-fat yogurt*

# Fruity Yogurt

*Babies about 8 months old and up will start expecting more from their food.
Simple mashes and purées will start to get boring, and many babies will let runny
food simply run back out of their mouths! Experiment with leaving chunkier
pieces of fruit in your baby's yogurt to see what he'll tolerate.*

* * * * *

1. Place yogurt in a bowl.

2. Remove the skin or peel from the fruit of your choice. Dice into small
   pieces, then fork-mash until smooth.

3. Stir into the yogurt, mixing until completely combined.

# Yogurt Popsicles

*Once your baby's proven her tolerance for plain yogurt popsicles, dress them up with
fruit! Mix mashed bananas, pears, or any other soft fruit into the yogurt before freezing.*

* * * * *

1. Stir the yogurt well.

2. Pour into clean popsicle molds, about ¾ of the way full

3. Place in the freezer and let freeze overnight.

**Freezing Techniques**
*If your popsicles aren't freezing well, don't put them in the freezer
door—opening and closing the door frequently will prevent an even
freeze. Make sure the freezer isn't overcrowded, because that will prevent the cold air from circulating. Also, freeze yogurt popsicles immediately after preparing them.*

# Cinnamon Applesauce Yogurt

**2 Servings**

½ cup plain whole-fat
    yogurt
¼ cup prepared or
    homemade applesauce
pinch of cinnamon

*You can make baby food from either raw or cooked apples. Raw apples are naturally crunchy and, when puréed, will turn into a meal with some texture. If your baby is resisting chunkier meals, cook the apples before puréeing. Cooking will essentially turn your apples into applesauce. However, when flavored with berries or cinnamon, it's still a fun, healthy meal for your baby.*

●　●　●　●　●

1. Stir the yogurt well to mix the creamy top layer with the rest of the yogurt.

2. Stir applesauce in with the yogurt.

3. Add a pinch of cinnamon and mix thoroughly.

4. Store leftovers in the refrigerator for up to 2 days.

**Yields 12 ounces**

1 pound fresh carrots
½ cup prepared or
 homemade apple juice

# Homemade Carrot-Apple Juice

*Carrot juice is loaded with antioxidants, so it's a very healthy drink for your baby.
For variety, try mixing in ½ cup pear juice. Other tasty flavors you could make
include carrot-peach juice or carrot-grape juice.*

•　•　•　•　•

1. Wash and scrub the carrots. Cut off both ends.

2. Push the carrots through a juicing machine, following the manufacturer's instructions. Catch the juice in a clean cup.

3. Mix in the apple juice, and stir thoroughly.

4. Refrigerate the leftovers, and use within 1–2 days.

**Yields 4 cups (1 liter)**

2 tablespoons sugar
¼ teaspoon baking soda
¼ teaspoon salt
4 cups water

# Electrolyte Drink

*When your baby has diarrhea or is vomiting, she quickly loses vital fluids. It's
important to replace those fluids with breastmilk or formula. You may also want
to supplement with a commercially prepared or homemade electrolyte drink,
which is easy on her tummy (if your pediatrician says it is all right).*

•　•　•　•　•

1. Place the water in a saucepan and boil for at least 10 minutes.

2. Mix the salt, baking soda, and sugar into the boiled water. Stir until completely dissolved. Add some orange juice, if you like, to improve their taste.

3. Store in the refrigerator for up to a day. Shake well before using.

# Homemade Apple Juice

*When making apple juice, look for apples that are, well, juicy! Red Delicious apples have a lot of juice, as do McIntosh, Winesap, and Granny Smith. Fresh apple juice takes time, but the results can be well worth the effort.*

* * * * *

**Yields ½ cup**

*2 fresh apples*
*⅛ teaspoon ascorbic acid*
*(vitamin C)*

1. Wash each apple well, and cut in half. Remove the peel, core, and seeds.

2. Run the apples through either an apple press or a juicer.

3. Pour the juice through a fine-mesh cheesecloth to remove any chunks.

4. Measure the juice you've produced. To keep it from turning brown and gathering sediment, add powdered ascorbic acid (vitamin C), in the proportion of 0.1 ounce of powder to 20 cups of juice. For ½ cup juice, you'd need to add only about ⅛ teaspoon of vitamin C.

5. Refrigerate immediately, and use within 1–2 days. If you want the juice to last longer (without turning into vinegar) you'll need to pasteurize it.

### Do-It-Yourself Pops
*When your baby's not feeling well, one of the most important things you can do for him is keep him hydrated. If he refuses to take an electrolyte drink from a bottle, try freezing it in ice-cube trays. Slide half of a popsicle stick into each cube once it is partially frozen so you have a convenient handle to use later.*

*2 cup grapes*
*6 cups water*

# Homemade Grape Juice

*Several different types of grapes make excellent juice. Concord grapes are particularly juicy, as are Bluebell and Valiant. Some juice grapes can also be used to make wine, but not always! Good grapes for wine-making include DeChaunac and Siebel.*

* * * * *

1. Wash the grapes thoroughly, removing any stems or blemished fruit. Mash them with a spoon or potato masher until you start to see the juice running out.

2. Place in a saucepan with the water. Bring to a boil; then simmer for 10–15 minutes. When cooked, strain the grapes and mash again.

3. Prepare another saucepan by draping 2 layers of cheesecloth over it. Secure the cloth to the pot with tape.

4. Pour the strained grapes over the cheesecloth; then allow to sit for about 12 hours (or overnight) in the refrigerator.

5. In the morning, discard the leftover fruit and cheesecloth. Run the juice through a fine-mesh strainer to remove any chunks. Refrigerate immediately, and use within 1–2 days.

**Some Like It Pulpy!**
*If you're making homemade juice to serve to a young baby, it's better to filter out all the pulp and chunky bits. For older children or grownups, though, feel free to add some of the fruit back in.*

# Fruit Yogurt Smoothie

*Why should the older children have all the cool summer drinks? As your baby gets older, she'll get more and more insistent upon having tastes of everything that everyone else consumes, including drinks! This is a recipe that the entire family can enjoy together.*

•  •  •  •  •

1. Peel the banana, removing any brown spots. Cut into chunks and place in food processor or blender.

2. Wash the strawberries and remove the stems. Cut in half and place in food processor.

3. Wash the peach and cut in half. Remove the pit and skin. Cut into chunks and add to the food processor.

4. Add the yogurt and purée until the smoothie is completely blended. Run through a fine sieve to remove any strawberry seeds.

**Substitute with Soy**
*If your child appears to have an allergy or intolerance to dairy products, feel free to substitute soy yogurt for regular. Make sure that your baby doesn't have a soy allergy—serve her regular soy yogurt alone before mixing it into a fruit smoothie.*

**4 Servings**

1 cup plain whole-fat yogurt
1 ripe banana
½ ripe peach
½ cup fresh or frozen strawberries

½ cup dry soybeans
2 cups water

# Homemade Soy Milk

*Soy milk is readily available, but you're often forced to buy fairly large containers. If you need a smaller amount of soy milk (and don't want to pay exorbitant prices for single-serving boxes), try making it yourself! Keep in mind that this shouldn't become a substitute for breastmilk or an iron-fortified infant formula.*

· · · · ·

1.  Rinse and drain the soybeans several times in cold water. Place into a pot, cover with water, and soak overnight in the refrigerator.

2.  In the morning, put the beans in a food processor with about 1½ cups water. Purée until smooth, about 4 minutes.

3.  Bring 4 tablespoons of water to a boil. Add the soybean purée and stir constantly until the mixture starts to foam.

4.  Pour the hot purée into a pressing bag or a very fine colander. Extrude the soy milk through the holes into a pot. When all of the milk has been extruded, heat the pot to boiling and cook for 6–7 minutes, stirring constantly.

5.  Remove the milk from the heat, and store in a sealing container. Serve warm or cold, depending on the baby's preference. Store in the refrigerator.

### It's All in the Taste

*While many "big people" like the taste of plain, unadulterated soy milk, children may balk because it doesn't have the richness of dairy milk, or the sweetness of fruit juice. Try adding a little sugar or artificial sweetener while the soy milk is still warm, stirring until it is completely dissolved, then chill. Be sure to shake or stir well before serving.*

# Hard-Boiled Egg Yolks

*Egg yolks are a great source of protein. They also have some vitamin A and iron. While they do have a lot of cholesterol, that's not something that you should worry about when feeding your baby. Just feed him a wide variety of foods, and you'll be fine.*

· · · · ·

1. Place the entire egg in a saucepan.

2. Pour cold water into the saucepan until the water is about 1 inch over the top of the egg. Cover and bring to a boil.

3. Reduce heat to a slow boil, and cook for an additional 12–14 minutes. Once done, drain the hot water and fill the saucepan with cold water to stop the egg from cooking. Let cool for 10–15 minutes.

4. Tap the egg lightly; then peel the shell off. Cut the egg in half and remove the white.

5. Mash the egg yolk with a fork. Add breastmilk or formula, 1 tablespoon at a time, until the egg is a creamy texture.

**No Leftovers**
*Freezing hard-boiled eggs isn't a great idea because eggs have such a high moisture content. Freezing eggs will considerably change the texture. It's better to simply cook one egg at a time for baby food.*

**1 Serving**

*1 egg*
*4 cups water*
*¼ cup breastmilk or formula*

# Egg Yolk Scramble

*Scrambling just the egg yolk can produce a dry, flaky result. If
your baby doesn't like the texture, try beating a little water
formula, or soy milk in with the egg yolk before cooking.*

· · · · ·

1. Crack the egg and separate out the yolk. Discard the white.

2. Whisk the yolk briskly in a bowl. Pour into a frying pan, adding a bit of margarine or oil, if not using a nonstick pan.

3. Scramble the egg until there is no visible liquid in the pan and the egg is completely cooked.

4. Mash with a fork and feed to your baby as finger food. Or, if she prefers, mix with a little breastmilk or formula to create a soupier meal.

# Poached Egg Yolks

*When adding egg yolk to your baby's diet, start slow. At first, offer just a
single bite of egg yolk, and see how she likes the taste and texture.
Gradually increase the amount of egg yolk you offer, but remember to
withhold egg whites until your baby's first birthday.*

· · · · ·

1. Crack the egg and separate out the yolk. Discard the white.

2. Bring the water to a boil in a medium saucepan.

3. Reduce the water to a simmer, and then slide in the egg yolk. Cook until firm, about 3–4 minutes.

4. Mash the egg yolk with a fork. Add breastmilk or formula, 1 tablespoon at a time, until the egg has a creamy texture.

# Silken Tofu Cubes

**1 Serving**

*½-inch square piece of tofu*

*Tofu comes in several densities, and is named according to its texture: extra firm, firm, soft, and silken. For your baby's first chewable tofu, try using silken. It's soft enough that it will dissolve easily in his mouth.*

•  •  •  •  •

1. Place the tofu on a plate.

2. Slice into small cubes, about ½-inch pieces.

3. Allow your baby to pick up the tofu and self-feed, under careful supervision to prevent choking.

### Chinese Versus Japanese Tofu

*There are two basic types of easily available tofu: Chinese and Japanese. Chinese tofu comes in extra-firm, firm, and soft. Japanese tofu is the silken variety; because of the way it's manufactured, it tends to be creamier and almost custard-like.*

1 package active dry yeast
4 cups all-purpose flour
4 tablespoons sugar
1½ tablespoons sugar
8 cups water
2 tablespoons oil
1 teaspoon salt, optional

# Homemade Bagels

*Bagels are the ultimate teething food: chewy enough to feel good on your baby's tender gums, nutritious, and big enough that she can't shove the whole thing in her mouth at once. Experiment with adding sesame or poppy seeds for other members of the family.*

◦　◦　◦　◦　◦

1. Preheat oven to 375°F. Pour the yeast, 1 tablespoon of flour, and 1 tablespoon sugar into a bowl along with 1 cup of warm water. Mix until dissolved; then allow it to sit for 10–15 minutes, or until the yeast forms a sponge.

2. Add in the rest of the flour, sugar, oil, and salt. Mix, adding flour if needed, until the dough is stiff. Cover and let the dough rise for about 15 minutes. While the dough is rising, fill a large saucepan with water and bring to a boil.

3. Split the dough into 12 balls. Poke a hole in each ball and round it out so that the hole stretches to about a 1-inch diameter. Drop into the boiling water in batches of three. Boil 2 minutes on each side, using tongs to flip the bagel over.

4. As each bagel comes out of the boiling pot, drain it briefly on paper towels. Place the bagels on a greased baking sheet, then bake for 20–25 minutes.

5. Allow bagels to cool completely. Supervise closely to make sure your baby doesn't bite off a large piece.

# 12–18 Months

# Apricot Rice

**2 Servings**

¼ cup brown rice
½ cup water
1 ripe apricot

*Once your baby starts to get more teeth, give your food processor a rest! Try pulsing the food just enough to mix it up, but stop short of completely liquefying her meals. Try preparing puréed food with more and more texture until she is ready for discrete pieces.*

●　●　●　●　●

1. Combine the rice with ½ cup water in a saucepan. Bring to a boil; then simmer for 20 minutes, or until all liquid has been absorbed.

2. Wash the apricot well. Peel it, remove the pit, and chop into small pieces.

3. Combine the rice and apricot in a food processor or blender. Pulse to desired consistency.

4. If making a thin mixture, purée until smooth. Add breastmilk or formula as needed to make the mixture creamier.

### Out-of-Season Apricots

*If apricots aren't in season, feel free to substitute canned apricots. Just try to find ones that aren't canned in heavy syrup, because that will add a lot of unwanted sugar or corn syrup to the dish. Look for fruit canned in natural juices only, or at least in light syrup. If not, use peaches, nectarines, or another stone fruit—your baby will never know the difference.*

## Corn Cereal

**2 Servings**

¼ cup ground corn
1 cup water

*Corn is a common allergen, so it shouldn't be introduced until your baby's first birthday. From that point on, you can experiment with different kinds of ground corn. Use the most finely ground corn you can find.*

•　•　•　•　•

1. Pour the water into a small saucepan. Bring to a rolling boil.

2. Add the finely ground corn into the boiling water, stirring constantly for about 1 minute.

3. Cover the pot, turn down the heat to low, and simmer for 8–10 minutes, or until the corn turns into a thick cereal. Stir occasionally to prevent sticking and burning.

4. If the corn cereal is too thick for your baby, thin it out with a bit of breastmilk or formula.

## Rice-Lentil Cereal

**3 Servings**

¼ cup white rice
⅛ cup lentils
⅛ cup chopped tomatoes
1 cup water

*Lentils and tomatoes go well together because the slightly acidic nature of the tomato balances the thick flavor of the beans. Just be sure that your baby hasn't shown any sign of allergy to tomatoes.*

•　•　•　•　•

1. Combine the lentils in a saucepan with the water. Bring to a boil; then cook at a rapid boil for 15 minutes.

2. Add the rice and tomatoes; then reduce to a simmer. Cook for another 25–30 minutes, or until all liquid is absorbed.

3. Once cool, fork-mash or purée the meal according to baby's preference. Thin with water, breastmilk, or formula if desired.

# Rice with Pears

*Cooked pears and rice is a great combination. Because the pears will cook to be quite soft, your toddler won't have any trouble chewing them along with the more-textured rice.*

* * * * *

**3 Servings**

*¼ cup white rice*
*½ ripe pear*
*½ cup water*

1. Remove skin and core from pear, and chop into small pieces. Pour the water into a small saucepan. Bring to a rolling boil.

2. Add the rice and pears; then reduce to a simmer. Cook for 25–30 minutes or until all liquid is absorbed.

3. Once cool, fork-mash or purée the meal according to baby's preference. Thin with water, breastmilk, or formula if desired.

## Too Much of a Good Thing

*Lentils are a great way to add protein and fiber to your baby's diet. Lentils and rice, when combined, make a complete protein, which will fill up and satisfy your baby in a healthy way. Don't go overboard, though! Introduce this recipe in small amounts at first, and watch for loose stools or other signs that he's had enough fiber for one day.*

## Boiled Rice with Milk

**2 Servings**

½ cup rice
1 cup water
1 cup milk (or soy milk)
3 tablespoons sugar

*Popular in India, this simple recipe insures that your baby gets both the carbohydrates (from rice) and the calcium (from milk) that she needs. You can use any kind of rice in this recipe. Just remember that brown rice will be thicker and chunkier than white rice, and will also take longer to cook.*

1. Put rice and water in pan. Heat to boil; then reduce heat and simmer until water is absorbed, about 20 minutes for white rice.

2. Once rice is cooked, add milk and sugar to the pan and mix well.

3. Cook at medium heat for 10 minutes, stirring often. Mixture will thicken.

4. Allow mixture to cool and mash with fork to desired consistency. Serve lukewarm.

## Kiwi Protein

**1 Serving**

1 ripe kiwi fruit
½ ripe banana
¼ cup cottage cheese

*Kiwi livens up any dish because of its vibrant green color and sweet flavor. It's also high in fiber, especially if your baby eats the seeds along with the fleshy fruit. To tell when a kiwi is ripe, squeeze it lightly. It'll give under pressure but won't fall apart.*

1. Trim the ends of the kiwi. Ease a spoon under the peel, going all the way around the fruit, until the fleshy center slides out. Cut into small pieces.

2. Peel the banana, removing any brown spots.

3. Combine the fruits on a plate. Add the cottage cheese, and fork-mash to desired consistency.

4. If the mixture has too much texture for your baby, add a little yogurt and continue fork-mashing until creamy.

# Baby Muesli

*Muesli, which means "mixture" in German, is a breakfast-type cereal that can actually be made of many different ingredients. It was first created by a Swiss nutritionist as a health food, and the exact content of the recipe varies. Feel free to substitute different fruits and grains.*

**2 Servings**

¼ cup regular oats (not quick-cooking)
1 ripe pear
2 ripe apricots
½ ripe banana
1 cup milk (or soy milk)

•   •   •   •   •

1. Peel the banana, pear, and apricots. Remove all stems, seeds, and pits. Chop into small pieces.

2. Pour the oats and milk into a saucepan. Bring to a boil; then cook at a boil for about 30 seconds.

3. Add in the fruit pieces and stir thoroughly.

4. Cover the pot, turn down the heat to low, and simmer for 8–10 minutes, or until the oats are smooth and thick. Stir occasionally to prevent sticking and burning.

5. Depending on your baby's preference, either serve as-is, or purée in a food processor for a creamier texture.

## Muesli Versus Granola

*Muesli is traditionally made of uncooked oats, though for babies you should cook the oats first. For older children or adults, however, you can make muesli by mixing uncooked oats with dried fruits and serving with milk. Granola, while still made primarily from oats, is usually baked with honey or other sweeteners to give it a sweet, crunchy taste.*

1 ripe banana
¼ cup light cream

# Creamed Bananas

*Creamed foods may be tasty, but they're not very good for your waistline. Even with babies and toddlers, limit the amount of creamed fruits and vegetables they eat to once or twice a week.*

•  •  •  •  •

1. Peel the banana, removing any brown spots. Cut into slices and place in food processor or blender.

2. Add cream.

3. Purée to desired consistency. If desired, add more cream to make a smoother purée.

4. If your baby likes his food with more texture, fork-mash instead of using the food processor.

### Sweeten the Deal
*For a 1-year-old, creamed fruit will be sweet enough all on its own. If you're trying to feed the leftovers to adults or older children, especially ones who balk at the idea of eating "baby food," try adding a pinch of sugar and cinnamon. This will make the dish taste a bit less bland, and a bit more grown-up.*

# Bananas and OJ

**1 Serving**

*1 ripe banana*
*1 medium juice orange*

*Bananas and orange juice make a great combination, nutrition-wise. Bananas are loaded with iron, while oranges are full of vitamin C. Getting your baby used to fruit is a great way to start her out on a healthy lifestyle. Watch out for citrus allergies as you introduce your child to oranges for the first time.*

•   •   •   •   •

1. Slice the orange in half. Juice it using either a juicing machine or a manual juicer. You can also simply squeeze firmly over a bowl. Strain out any pulp or seeds.

2. Peel the banana, removing any brown spots. Cut into slices and place on a plate.

3. Fork-mash the banana, slowly adding in the orange juice. Continue mashing until the texture is such that your baby can eat it with a spoon.

## Too Soupy!
*Add too much liquid to a puréed fruit meal? If your baby is older than a year, try adding a bit of yogurt (soy or milk) to thicken it. Or, if you have a bit of leftover baby rice or baby oatmeal, mix that in—it makes a great instant thickener.*

**4 Servings**

1 pint fresh strawberries
1 large banana
10 large fresh mint leaves

# Minted Bananas and Strawberries

*Bananas and strawberries are always a winning combination, but how about livening them up with a touch of mint? Instead of the fresh mint leaves in this recipe, you can substitute ¼ teaspoon dried mint, which you've soaked in 1 teaspoon water or apple juice concentrate for 2 hours.*

•  •  •  •  •

1. Rinse strawberries and remove hulls (leaves and central core) with a sharp knife. Cut into pieces.

2. Peel banana, removing any brown spots. Cut into pieces.

3. With a sharp knife, cut the mint leaves into thin strips.

4. Place all ingredients in a steamer basket. Place in a pot over about 2 inches of water. Bring to a boil, and steam for about 5 minutes.

5. Serve in pieces, or mash to desired consistency.

**Which Mint?**
*Mint leaves are a great ingredient to add a refreshing taste to everything from lemonade to fruit. You can easily grow mint yourself in your garden or in a pot, or buy fresh leaves at the store in the fresh herb section. If you grow mint yourself, you can choose from peppermint, spearmint, and other varieties.*

# Steamed Grapes and Squash

*Have you ever tried cooking grapes? They add a great taste when paired with butternut squash. Steaming grapes makes them more tender and less of a choking hazard. In addition, you don't need to peel them. You should still supervise your child closely when eating any kind of grapes.*

**5 Servings**

*1 medium butternut squash
15–20 large, seedless green grapes*

●　●　●　●　●

1. Wash squash. Peel, remove seeds, and cut into 1-inch cubes.

2. Place squash in a steamer basket. Place in pot over about 2 inches of water. Bring to a boil and steam for about 6 minutes.

3. Wash the grapes. Cut in half, if desired.

4. Add grapes to steamer basket and steam for another 6 minutes, or until tender when pricked with a fork.

5. Serve in pieces, or mash to desired consistency.

## Bananas with Papaya and Mango

**5 Servings**

1 small ripe papaya
1 large ripe mango
2 ripe bananas

*This tropical treat pairs bananas, a favorite food of many babies, with two other tropical fruits, papaya and mango. This combination is full of potassium and vitamin C, and is sweet and tasty for your baby. Try to match the size of the papaya and the mango—choose a small papaya and a large mango.*

* * * * *

1. Slice papaya in half and remove seeds and skin. Cut into small chunks.

2. Remove skin and pit from mango, and cut into small chunks.

3. Peel bananas and cut into slices.

4. Place papaya in a steamer basket, and steam for about 5 minutes. Add mango and banana, steam for another 5 minutes, or until very tender.

5. Serve in pieces, or mash to desired consistency.

### Mango Tips

*Slicing a mango can be tricky. If the fruit is tender and ripe, it's almost impossible to eat a mango without making a huge mess. One tip is to slice both "cheeks" off the mango—cut off the rounded parts on both sides of the pit. Then with a sharp knife, cut squares in the flesh while still on the skin, push the skin inside out, and slice off the squares. Then dice what's left of the mango off the pit.*

# Artichoke Leaves

**2 Servings**

*1 artichoke*

*An artichoke may look daunting, but they're actually fairly easy to cook and eat. They make a fun finger food for toddlers, too, because you get to pick the leaves off the artichoke and chew on the bottoms. When selecting artichokes, look for ones that are bright green, crisp, and tightly closed.*

●　●　●　●　●

1.  With a sharp knife, cut off the artichoke stem near base.

2.  Using kitchen scissors, cut the thorn off each artichoke leaf. Cut each leaf about ½ inch down from the tip. Use a knife to slice across the central core to cut off the tips of the leaves in the central portion.

3.  Place the artichoke in a steamer basket over about 3 inches of water. Steam for 35–40 minutes, or until the bottom leaves can be easily removed.

4.  To eat, remove one leaf at a time. Pull leaf between your teeth, scraping the tender flesh off with your bottom teeth. Watch toddlers at all times to make sure they are only eating the bottom of each leaf—discard the rest.

5.  When you've eaten all the leaves, use a knife to scrape the "choke," the fuzzy part, off the artichoke heart (the tender middle portion). Eat the heart.

### Artichoke Trivia
*Artichokes are members of the thistle family, which may explain the thorns and the fuzzy choke in the middle. Artichokes also have a unique characteristic—they contain natural chemicals that make everything you eat immediately afterward taste sweet! This is yet another reason for toddlers with a sweet tooth to try artichokes.*

**2 Servings**

1 apple
½ cup water
¼ cup milk (or soy milk)

# Mashed Cooked Apples with Milk

*Apples are one of the simplest fruits for your baby to enjoy, and they're available all year-round! For this recipe, pick firm, sweet apples like Yellow Delicious, Fuji, or McIntosh. Apples that are more tart, like Granny Smith, will also work, but you may want to add a little sugar to the final product before serving it.*

•  •  •  •  •

1. Peel and core the apple, and cut into 1-inch pieces.

2. Place apple pieces in small pan with water—water should almost cover apple pieces. Add a little more water if necessary.

3. Bring to a boil; then simmer over low heat until apple pieces are tender, about 10 minutes. Check while cooking to make sure that there is still water left, and add more water while cooking if necessary.

4. When cooked, remove apples from heat. If there is a lot of excess water, drain off.

5. Add milk to pot and mash with a fork or potato masher until desired consistency, mixing well.

### Choosing Apples

*Try moving beyond the typical grocery store apple varieties of Granny Smith, Yellow Delicious, and Red Delicious. Some good types to try are Fuji, Braeburn, McIntosh, Gala, Pippin, Pink Lady, and other local varieties. Try your local farmer's market for apples that are in season— you'll be amazed at how much better they taste!*

# Cottage Cheese and Cooked Fruit

**2 Servings**

½ cup cottage cheese
½ peach
4 strawberries
¼ cup water

*Cottage cheese is a versatile and tasty treat, with less sugar than flavored yogurts. Try pairing it with your favorite fruits. This recipe calls for a mixture of peaches and strawberries, but cottage cheese is equally good with other raw or cooked fruits like blueberries, pears, or pineapple. For a savory taste, try cottage cheese with salad dressing such as Thousand Island.*

●　●　●　●　●

1. Peel peach, remove pit, and cut into pieces.

2. Remove hull and stem from strawberries and cut into quarters.

3. Place strawberries and peaches in microwave-safe glass dish. Add water and cover loosely with lid or with microwave-safe plastic wrap.

4. Microwave on high for 2 minutes. Remove cover carefully and stir. If fruit is not soft, recover and heat until soft, 30 seconds at a time. Let cooked fruit cool to lukewarm.

5. Place cottage cheese in bowl. Pour cooked strawberries and peaches on top, including juices.

### All about Cottage Cheese
*Cottage cheese comes in many varieties—small curd, large curd, low-fat, low-salt, and others. For babies and young children, choose the higher fat varieties. Cottage cheese has a fair amount of salt in it, but avoid the low-sodium types—salt is necessary for the curdling process that makes cottage cheese, so the low-salt varieties tend not to taste very good.*

# Lima Beans

**2 Servings**

¼ cup lima beans (fresh or frozen)

2 cups water or chicken stock

*Lima beans, also called butter beans, are a great source of fiber. They have a sweet taste that many babies like right away. To counteract the fiber, though, be sure to offer in small amounts, or combine with a binding fruit such as bananas.*

*  *  *  *  *

1. Rinse the lima beans.

2. Bring the water or chicken stock to a boil. Add lima beans.

3. Reduce heat and simmer for 25–30 minutes, or until beans are completely tender.

4. Fork-mash to desired consistency, or serve as finger food.

# Scrambled Eggs with Wheat Germ

**1 Serving**

1 egg

½ tablespoon wheat germ

*Give your baby's eggs a nutty flavor by adding wheat germ. She'll also be getting extra doses of vitamin E and folic acid.*

*  *  *  *  *

1. Crack the egg into a bowl. Beat thoroughly while stirring in the wheat germ.

2. Pour the egg into a medium-hot nonstick frying pan, adding a bit of oil or butter if the egg starts to stick.

3. Scramble the egg. Let cool before serving.

# Scrambled Eggs with Cheese

*Use a mild cheese in this recipe, especially if your baby hasn't had a wide variety of cheeses yet. Mozzarella melts particularly well, as does Monterey jack or a mild Cheddar. Avoid sharp cheeses until your baby is more used to them.*

**1 Serving**

*1 egg*
*1 tablespoon milk (regular or soy)*
*2 tablespoons grated cheese*

•   •   •   •   •

1. Crack the egg into a bowl and add milk. Beat thoroughly.

2. Pour the egg into a medium-hot non-stick frying pan, adding a bit of oil or butter if the egg starts to stick.

3. Scramble the egg, adding the cheese about halfway through. Continue scrambling until the egg is cooked and cheese melted.

### Cooking with Milk

*It's safe to cook with milk as long as you're using pasteurized milk. It's safe to scald milk (heat to just below the boiling point), but you don't want to actually boil it—boiling causes a skinlike layer to form on the surface. Always make sure your milk tastes and smells fresh before serving it to your baby.*

**1 Serving**

*1 egg*
*1 tablespoon milk*
*1 tablespoon cottage cheese*

# Scrambled Egg Whites with Cottage Cheese

*Adding cottage cheese to eggs tends to make them lighter and fluffier, especially if you use the small-curd cottage cheese. The curd size is more important than the fat content. You can use regular or low-fat cottage cheese, depending on what the rest of your family is eating.*

＊　＊　＊　＊　＊

1. Crack the egg into an egg separator. Keep the white; discard the yolk.

2. Whisk the egg white and milk together. Once mixed, whisk in cottage cheese, stirring until it is completely mixed in.

3. Pour the egg into a medium-hot nonstick frying pan, adding a bit of oil or butter if the egg starts to stick.

4. Scramble the egg and cheese until cooked. Allow to cool before serving.

**1 Serving**

*1 tortilla*
*1 tablespoon cream cheese*
*1 thin slice of cheese*

# Cream Cheese Tortilla Rollups

*You can use either flour or corn tortillas for this recipe. Use corn as long as your baby shows no allergy to corn, or flour if he doesn't have a wheat allergy. Flour tortillas are slightly higher in calories and fat, but may roll up more easily.*

＊　＊　＊　＊　＊

1. Lay the tortilla out on a microwaveable plate.

2. Spread a thin layer of cream cheese over the tortilla.

3. Lay a thin slice of cheese (American, Swiss, or any other hard cheese that your baby likes) in the middle of the tortilla.

4. Roll up and warm in the microwave for about 10–15 seconds.

5. Cut into small slices and serve as finger food.

# Carrot Omelet

**1 Serving**

1 egg
1 small carrot
1 tablespoon milk or water
½ tablespoon butter or
    margarine

*It may be tempting to start seasoning your baby's omelets with salt and pepper, but there's no need to. Your child isn't used to heavily seasoned food, so let her enjoy the food's natural flavors. She'll have plenty of time for herbs and spices later.*

● ● ● ● ●

1. Wash and peel the carrot. Grate about 2 tablespoons.

2. Crack the egg into a bowl and add milk or water. Beat thoroughly.

3. Add grated carrot and stir completely.

4. Melt the butter or margarine in a nonstick frying pan. Pour in the egg mixture and tilt the pan to spread evenly.

5. When the egg is set, flip to cook the other side. When the egg is cooked through, remove from heat.

6. Cool to lukewarm, and cut into pieces to serve as finger food or to be eaten with a baby-safe fork.

### Grate or Dice?

*Finally your baby is starting to eat some of the same foods that the grownups do! But not quite. For recipes like omelets that contain vegetables, always grate the veggies rather than dice. Most new eaters are prone to choking, and your baby's already got a lot to deal with when she first tackles the texture of an omelet. Help her out by finely grating the vegetables.*

**3 Servings**

½ small zucchini
½ medium carrot
1 small onion
2 eggs
3 cups water
¼ cup milk
¼ cup grated cheese
1 tablespoon butter or oil

# Vegetable Frittata

*Dress up this recipe with a crunchy topping, if your baby's developmentally ready for it. You can make your own bread crumbs by toasting whole-wheat bread, then running it through a food processor or blender. Sprinkle bread crumbs over the frittata, dribble a bit of melted butter on top, and bake.*

•  •  •  •  •

1.  Preheat the oven to 350°F.

2.  Remove the peel from the onion and carrot. Wash and grate the zucchini, onion, and carrots, about ¼ cup of each. Melt the butter in a saucepan, and sauté the vegetables for 8–10 minutes, or until completely softened.

3.  Crack the eggs into a small bowl. Whisk together with the milk and cheese, and mix in the vegetables.

4.  Place the eggs and vegetables into a greased baking pan. Bake for 35–40 minutes, or until the eggs are completely cooked.

5.  Once cool, serve to your baby in small pieces or fork-mash to desired consistency.

# Simple French Toast

**3 Servings**

*1 egg*
*3 slices whole-wheat bread*
*1 tablespoon milk or water*
*1 tablespoon oil*
*1 teaspoon white sugar*
*pinch of cinnamon*

*French toast is not really a French food. By most accounts, it originated in the United States hundreds of years ago. Some think the original French toast was made by soaking toasted French bread in a mixture of wine and orange juice. Tasty, perhaps, but definitely not for your baby!*

* * * * *

1. Combine the egg, milk, sugar, and cinnamon in a medium bowl. Beat thoroughly.

2. Heat oil in a large frying pan. One at a time, dip the bread slices into the egg mixture and soak for about 10 seconds. Flip the bread over and soak on the other side.

3. Place each of the bread slices into the heated pan.

4. Fry on each side until lightly browned, usually 1–3 minutes per side.

5. Let cool completely before cutting into pieces and serving as finger food.

## Dress It Up!

*Once your baby has mastered simple French toast, try adding fruit to make it a bit more appealing to the rest of the family. Mix a few mashed blueberries or strawberries into the egg mixture, for example. Or, if you want to try a creamier French toast, add a little applesauce to the egg mixture. You can also add a little vanilla or almond extract.*

½ cup plain or vanilla
    yogurt
1 tablespoon blueberries

# Yogurt with Blueberries

*Yogurt with fruit is a great "teaching food" because it gives babies the chance to deal with smooth textures, plus lumpier pieces, all in one dish. If your baby chokes on the berries, slice them into smaller pieces and remind him to chew. Demonstrate the chewing action, and see if he'll copy you with a bite in his mouth.*

●　●　●　●　●

1. Mix the yogurt thoroughly.

2. Wash the blueberries well. Cut each one into quarters.

3. Sprinkle blueberries over the top. Use fresh blueberries; the frozen kind are good for cooking but become soggy when thawed.

4. Allow your baby to self-feed under careful supervision.

### Get the Blender Back Out
*If your baby doesn't seem quite ready for discrete pieces of berries mixed into his food, don't be afraid to dust off the food processor. Learning to chew his food is a process, and some babies get the hang of it sooner than others. When it doubt, purée.*

# Cheese Squares

*Baked cheese squares are a delicious way to get some extra protein in your child. Be patient while this finger food is baking—it may take longer than you think.*

●   ●   ●   ●   ●

1. Preheat the oven to 350°F.

2. Shred the cheese into a medium bowl.

3. Add the egg, flour, and cottage cheese. Stir well.

4. Place into a greased baking dish.

5. Bake for about 45 minutes, or until a toothpick in the middle comes out clean. Cool and cut into squares.

**4 Servings**

*1 cup all-purpose flour*
*1 egg*
*3 ounces Mozzarella, Cheddar, or Monterey Jack cheese*
*1 cup cottage cheese*

# Mashed Avocado and Cottage Cheese

*Cottage cheese is a relative of pot cheese or farmer's cheese; these varieties are basically cottage cheese that has been pressed. They are very similar to Queso Blanco, a white cheese that is produced by pressing the whey out of cottage cheese. As your baby gets older, introduce more variety into her diet by experimenting with these other types of cottage cheese.*

●   ●   ●   ●   ●

1. Cut a small slice of avocado and remove the peel. Fork-mash on a plate.

2. Combine with the cottage cheese and continue fork-mashing until the mixture is at the desired consistency.

3. If the mix is still too chunky, try fork-mashing in some yogurt, breastmilk, or formula.

**1 Serving**

*1 ripe avocado*
*½ cup cottage cheese*

## Fruity Cream

**2 Servings**

½ cup heavy cream
2 tablespoons sugar
½ cup sour cream
½ cup yogurt
4 strawberries or ¼ cup
   blueberries

*There are several approaches to Fruity Cream. This recipe is for a cream sauce that can be spread over soft fruit. Another method is to purée your fruit first, add equal amounts of water and sugar, mix well with a small amount of cream, and freeze.*

•　•　•　•　•

1. Pour the cream into a medium metal bowl. Using an egg beater or electric mixer, whip until soft peaks are formed.

2. Fold in the sour cream, yogurt, and sugar until completely mixed.

3. Refrigerate until ready for use.

4. Serve to your baby over a small dish of washed and chopped strawberries, blueberries, or other soft fruit.

## Banana Milk

**1 Serving**

1 ripe banana
½ cup milk (regular or soy)

*Serve this drink immediately, because it may start to turn brown if it's refrigerated for more than a few hours. If you're making a large batch for the rest of the family, consider adding a bit of maple syrup as a sweetener.*

•　•　•　•　•

1. Peel the banana and remove any brown spots. Cut into slices and place into the food processor or blender.

2. Add milk. Purée until completely smooth.

3. Pour the mixture through a cheesecloth or strainer to remove any lumpy bits of banana.

4. Serve to your baby in a sippy cup as a refreshing beverage.

# Cottage Cheese and Pea Mash

**1 Serving**

¼ cup peas (fresh or frozen)
1 cup water
½ cup cottage cheese

*If your baby is already gumming down cottage cheese and peas separately, this is one of the easiest recipes you can make! Quick to make and entirely healthy, your baby can feel good about feeding himself. Parents will feel great about getting a rest while their baby self-feeds (or, in some cases, feeds the floor).*

•   •   •   •   •

1.  Wash the peas and place in a saucepan with water. Bring to a boil, then simmer for about 10 minutes, or until peas are very tender.

2.  Allow peas to cool; then combine on a plate with the cottage cheese.

3.  Fork-mash to desired consistency, or let your baby pick up individual peas and pieces of large-curd cottage cheese by himself.

### Shopping for Milk

*Of the types of milk available in most grocery stores, the common varieties are whole, reduced-fat, low-fat, and nonfat. For children under 2, stick to whole milk, continue to breastfeed, or give your child a toddler formula, because babies this age generally do not need a reduced-fat diet. For children over 2, you can gradually switch to reduced-fat (2%) or low-fat milk (1%).*

½ *pound of flour*
2 *eggs*
*pinch of salt*

# Homemade Egg Pasta

*Get out the elbow grease for making your own pasta! Store-bought pastas are generally enriched with a variety of minerals and vitamins. However, if you want your baby to have only fresh pasta with no additives, making it yourself is the way to go.*

●　●　●　●　●

1. Mix the flour and salt together and put the flour in a pile on a clean surface. Use your fingers to make a well in the middle of the flour pile.

2. Crack the eggs into the well and mix with a fork, gradually pulling in flour from the well. When your dough begins to come together, knead for 10–12 minutes, or until you have a smooth dough. Add a teaspoon of water only if necessary—almost none should be needed.

3. Flour your work surface and roll out the dough until it becomes a nearly transparent sheet. Flip and reflour the surface as necessary.

4. Slice into strands if making spaghetti and cut into squares if using for ravioli or other shaped pasta.

5. To cook, bring a large pot of water to a boil and cook for 4–5 minutes, or until pasta floats to the top of the pot (much shorter cooking time than store-bought pasta).

# Regular Pasta

*Don't rinse pasta before serving to your baby. The starch in the cooking water will make the pasta a little bit sticky, which is perfect for young fingers.*

＊ ＊ ＊ ＊ ＊

1. Bring the water to a rapid boil in a large saucepan.

2. Add pasta and stir to separate the noodles. Continue boiling for 10–12 minutes, or according to package directions. Pasta should be soft and completely cooked.

3. Let cool completely; then cut into ½-inch-long pieces for your baby to pick up and self-feed.

**1 Serving**

¼ cup Homemade Egg Pasta (page 136), or boxed spaghetti, or other pasta
4 cups of water

¼ cup Homemade Egg
   Pasta (page 136) or
   boxed wide spaghetti
4 cups water
½ tablespoon butter or
   margarine

# Buttered Noodles

*If your child has any lactose allergy or sensitivity, stay away from butter. Use a lactose-free margarine, which is made from vegetable oil instead of cream. Some margarines are made with whey, so read the ingredients carefully.*

•   •   •   •   •

1.  Bring the water to a rapid boil in a large saucepan.

2.  Add pasta and stir to separate the noodles. Continue boiling for 10–12 minutes, or according to package directions. Pasta should be soft and completely cooked.

3.  Drain the pasta and return to the pot, cooking over very low heat. Add the butter and toss until completely melted.

4.  Cut into ½-inch-long pieces for baby to pick up and self-feed.

### Cook It Well

*While you may prefer your pasta al dente, undercooked noodles tend to cause young babies to choke. She's not after the perfect sauce or perfect noodle; she just wants something she can mash easily with her gums. Taste pasta before serving and err on the side of overcooking when it comes to pasta.*

# Noodles with Cheese

*Pasta comes in many different shapes, so it's perfectly acceptable to veer from the traditional macaroni! Experiment with conchiglie (shells), farfalle (bow ties), fusilli (twists), rotelle (wagon wheels), or any other fun shape your child might like.*

* * * * *

### 3 Servings

¾ cup elbow macaroni (or other shape)
4 cups water
2 tablespoons butter
2 tablespoons all-purpose flour
1½ cups milk
¾ cup grated cheese

1. Bring the water to a rapid boil in a large saucepan.

2. Add the macaroni, stirring to break up the pasta. Cook for 12–15 minutes, or until noodles are completely tender. Drain.

3. In a small saucepan, melt the butter over low heat. Stir in the flour, whisking constantly until it's dissolved. Add milk and cheese, stirring constantly, until it thickens into a sauce.

4. Pour the cheese sauce into the noodles, tossing to mix.

5. Allow to cool before serving to your baby.

### Choosing a Cheese

*For basic macaroni and cheese, try using Cheddar, Colby, or Monterey jack cheese. Mozzarella melts very well on pizza, but isn't great for cooking into a baby's meal because it tends to congeal rapidly. Experiment with different kinds of cheeses to see which kind your baby likes the best!*

# Egg Noodles with Peas

*Egg noodles are typically firmer than regular pasta. They're usually in the form of flat, wide noodles and are great for baking into casseroles. They hold up well with peas, and served together they provide a nice texture complement.*

· · · · ·

1. Bring the water to a rapid boil in a large saucepan.

2. Add pasta and peas. Stir to separate the noodles.

3. Continue boiling for 10–12 minutes, or according to package directions. Pasta should be soft and completely cooked.

4. Drain the pasta and peas, allowing to cool completely.

5. Cut the noodles into ½-inch-long pieces for baby to pick up and self-feed. Can be served with a tablespoon of grated cheese.

# Baby Ratatouille

*Ratatouille is a French vegetable stew. As shown here, this recipe can be cooked on the stove, but it's also a fantastic slow cooker meal. Microwaving is also acceptable, although the vegetables won't have the chance to simmer together and the flavors will not be as developed.*

· · · · ·

1. Heat the oil in a medium saucepan. Sauté onion until it begins to brown and turns translucent.

2. Add the eggplant, zucchini, and tomatoes into the saucepan. Bring to a boil; then reduce to a simmer.

3. Cook for 20 minutes. Stir in the herbs; then cook for another 20 minutes. Allow to cool; then fork-mash before serving.

# Creamy Coconut Lentils

*Coconut and lentils provide a new blend of tastes that your baby is sure to enjoy. No time like the present to wake up her taste buds! To increase the chances of her taking kindly to this new dish, be sure to use a mild curry and go easy on the onions.*

**3 Servings**

½ cup lentils
1 teaspoon curry powder
1 cup water
¼ small onion, diced
3 tablespoons coconut, shredded
¼ cup milk (regular or soy)

• • • • •

1. Bring the water to a rapid boil in a medium saucepan.

2. Add lentils, onions, and coconut, and reduce water to a simmer. Cook for about 45 minutes, or until the lentils are completely soft.

3. Add the milk and curry powder, and cook about another 15 minutes.

4. Allow to cool; then fork-mash before serving.

## Coconut Facts

*High in potassium and fiber, coconut is a nutritious food that many babies like. According to some research, coconuts also have medicinal value in fighting off infection and fungi, and may even help prevent various diseases. Coconut is high in saturated fat, but okay for babies to have on an occasional basis.*

## Chickpea Stew

**4 Servings**

1 cup canned chickpeas
2 medium tomatoes, diced
½ teaspoon cumin
2 cups chicken stock
   or water
1¼ cup parsley, chopped
¼ teaspoon lemon juice
¼ teaspoon sugar

*Chickpea (garbanzo bean) stew is a Middle Eastern favorite, and there's no reason it can't become a healthy part of your baby's repertoire. The earlier you introduce spices such as cumin, the more likely your child is to accept new flavors as he's growing up.*

•  •  •  •  •

1. Rinse the chickpeas and combine with tomatoes in a medium saucepan. Add stock or water and bring to a boil.

2. Add cumin, lemon juice, sugar, and parsley. Simmer for about 30 minutes, or until chickpeas are soft.

3. Allow to cool, then fork-mash before serving.

### Spice It Up

*Once your baby is at least 1 year old, consider serving a modified version of original Middle Eastern dishes. Add a little curry and turmeric and see how your child likes it. Also, for extra flavor, try using chicken stock instead of water for cooking the beans—just be sure to use stock you make yourself and not bouillon cubes, which contain too much sodium for an infant, and often contain other preservatives and flavor enhancers.*

# Red Lentil Dhal

*Dhal is an Indian lentil dish, and it's a traditional food served in many parts of the world. There are many different types of dhal, including mung dhal (which uses mung lentils), chana dhal (made with yellow lentils), and masoor dhal (split red lentils).*

●  ●  ●  ●  ●

1. Peel garlic and ginger. Push both through a press, or chop finely.

2. Bring the water to a rapid boil in a medium saucepan. Add lentils, onions, ginger, garlic, chili, and cumin, and reduce heat to a simmer.

3. Cook for about 45 minutes, or until the lentils are completely soft.

4. Allow to cool; then fork-mash before serving.

### Types of Lentils

*There are more than 150 variations of lentils out there. The most commonly available tend to be green, red, and brown lentils. They vary from country to country, but lentils are widely available throughout North America. Green lentils are particularly popular and have a mild flavor, which is good for your baby!*

**3 Servings**

½ cup split red lentils
2 cups chicken stock
   or water
½ teaspoon cumin
¼ small onion, diced
¼ mild green chili, diced
¼ teaspoon ginger
¼ teaspoon garlic

**2 Servings**

½ cup carrots
½ cup broccoli
½ cup peas (fresh or frozen)
4 cups water
¼ cup Cheddar, shredded

# Cheesy Vegetable Mash

*Mashed vegetables are extremely easy to make, and there's no law stating which vegetables go well together. Feel free to substitute with whatever is in season. Make sure to cook thoroughly, and always ensure that the vegetables are soft enough to be mashed with your baby's gums.*

•   •   •   •   •

1. Wash, peel, and cut the carrots into small pieces.

2. Wash the broccoli thoroughly, remove the stem, and cut into small florets.

3. Bring the water to a boil. Add carrots, broccoli, and peas, reduce heat to a simmer, and cook for about 25 minutes, or until carrots are soft. Drain the vegetables, then return to the saucepan.

4. Melt the cheese in a microwaveable dish, then pour over the vegetables. Mix thoroughly to coat.

5. Allow to cool; then fork-mash before serving.

# Dried Bean Stew

**4 Servings**

¼ cup dried lima beans
¼ cup dried black beans
4 cups water
½ cup tomato sauce
1 small potato
½ cup ham, diced

*A variation on the Indian dhal recipes, bean stew allows for more variety. If your family is partial to split peas, for example, feel free to use those instead. Any sort of meat can be substituted for the ham, and of course the meat can be omitted entirely for vegetarian families. The beans provide plenty of protein as is!*

•  •  •  •  •

1. Wash the dried beans. Place in a large saucepan with enough water to cover them. Soak overnight in the refrigerator

2. In the morning, drain the soaking water and refill with fresh water, about 3 inches over the top of the beans. Bring to a boil; then simmer for about 1 hour.

3. Wash and peel the potato. Dice into small pieces; then add to the cooking pot.

4. Add in the tomato sauce and ham. Continue simmering until potatoes are cooked, about another 45 minutes.

5. Allow to cool;, then fork-mash before serving.

## Beyond Kidney Beans

*Dried beans come in all shapes and sizes. Aside from chickpeas and kidney beans, there are fava beans, Great Northern beans, mung beans, pinto beans, soybeans, and many more varieties. They all take slightly different cooking times, but most benefit from an overnight soak—it will cut your cooking time in half, and makes for more tender beans.*

*1 cup canned chickpeas*
*1 tablespoon tahini*
*1 teaspoon lemon juice*
*1 teaspoon olive oil*
*1 teaspoon cumin*
*1 tablespoon water*
*1 clove garlic, optional*

# Simple Hummus

*Hummus is a classic Middle Eastern dish that can be served in a variety of ways. While serving it on pita bread is traditional, be flexible! Spread it on toast, or have your baby dip a cracker (or even a finger) into a dish of hummus.*

•   •   •   •   •

1.  If using garlic, peel it.

2.  Rinse the precooked chickpeas. Place in food processor or blender and purée completely. Add the garlic and purée until well chopped and smooth.

3.  Add the olive oil, tahini, cumin, and lemon juice. Continue puréeing for about a minute, scraping down the sides of the bowl as necessary.

4.  Add enough water to make a smooth paste. Purée until smooth.

### Tahini

*Tahini is a Middle Eastern sesame-seed paste. You can find it in a can in the international or Middle Eastern food section of your grocery store. Once you open the can, mix it well. Store the can in your refrigerator after opening. You can make tahini sauce by mixing equal amounts of water and tahini paste with a little lemon juice. This dipping sauce is tasty for falafel, vegetables, and other foods.*

# Broccoli with Oranges and Almonds

*A great way to serve vegetables: mix them with sweet fruit! Even fussy eaters will find something they like in this broccoli dish, which combines fruit with broccoli and nuts.*

* * * * *

**3 Servings**

½ head of broccoli
¼ cup sliced almonds
½ orange
2 tablespoons butter
4 cups water

1. Wash the broccoli and remove the stem. Dice into small florets.

2. Heat butter in a medium saucepan. Toast the almonds for about 5 minutes, or until lightly browned.

3. Bring water to a boil. Add broccoli and cook for about 15 minutes, or until broccoli is tender.

4. Slice the orange in half and remove the fruit with a grapefruit spoon. Cut into small pieces. Toss cooked broccoli, almonds, and oranges together.

5. If the textures are too challenging, omit the almonds and purée the broccoli and orange, adding breastmilk or formula as necessary to thin the mixture.

## 3 Servings

1 medium carrot, diced
½ medium sweet potato, diced
½ cup Cheddar
3 cups water

# Sweet Potato, Carrot, and Cheese Mash

*Always serve pasteurized cheese to infants. Pasteurization uses heat to kill bacteria, and pasteurized milks and cheeses are the safest way to introduce dairy products to children. While some contend that aged raw cheeses are safe to eat, these varieties are not yet FDA approved.*

●  ●  ●  ●  ●

1. Bring water to a boil in a medium saucepan. Add the sweet potato and the carrot, reduce to a simmer, and cook for 35 minutes, or until vegetables are tender. Grate the cheese.

2. Drain the vegetables and return to the saucepan. Over low heat, add in the grated cheese and stir until melted.

3. Allow to cool; then fork-mash before serving.

### Soft or Hard?

*Children's tastes for cheese run the gamut. Soft cheese include cream cheese and ricotta; these are great when spread on toast. Semi-soft cheeses like Monterey jack or Mozzarella are favorites for pizza. The hard cheeses (Cheddar, Swiss, Parmesan) are great for cooking or baking. Try experimenting with different varieties to find a kind that your baby, and the rest of your family, loves.*

# Lentils with Butternut Squash

*The richness of squash in this recipe combines well with the savory bell pepper and the protein-filled lentils. Children will like the sweetness from the squash and the orange juice.*

* * * * *

**3 Servings**

1 small bell pepper
½ butternut squash
½ cup lentils
½ teaspoon cinnamon
4 cups water
2 tablespoons orange juice

1. Rinse the lentils and place in a pot with the water. Bring to a boil.

2. Wash the pepper and remove the seeds. Dice into small pieces and add to lentils.

3. Wash the squash and slice in half. Peel the squash and remove the seeds. Dice into pieces, and add to the lentils.

4. Add the cinnamon and continue cooking for 40 minutes, or until lentils are completely tender.

5. Allow to cool; then fork-mash with orange juice before serving.

# Spinach with Cheese Sauce

*If your baby has a lactose allergy or intolerance, feel free to substitute with vegan cheeses. But beware: they are not all created equal. Many nondairy cheeses tend to melt rather poorly. Stick to brands that say "meltable," and try a small piece before attempting to melt an entire package.*

* * * * *

**2 Servings**

1 cup spinach (fresh or
   frozen)
½ cup Cheddar, grated
2 tablespoons all-purpose
   flour
2 tablespoons butter
⅛ teaspoon dry mustard
2 cups water
1 cup milk (regular or soy)

1. Bring the water to a boil in a medium saucepan. Add spinach and cook until tender.

2. In a separate small saucepan, melt the butter over low heat. Add the flour and mustard, stirring for 2–3 minutes, or until dissolved.

3. Add the milk, stirring constantly, and bring the mixture just to a boil. Stir in the cheese and cook until melted.

4. Mix the spinach into the cheese sauce. Allow to cool before serving.

## Broccoli and Cornmeal

**2 Servings**

¼ cup cornmeal
½ small head broccoli
3 cups water

*Cornmeal is simply ground corn. It's the main ingredient in staples such as polenta, Johnny bread, or cornbread, and babies often enjoy the sweet flavor of the corn.*

●　●　●　●　●

1.  Wash the broccoli and remove all stems. Cut into small florets.

2.  Bring 2 cups of water to a boil. Add the broccoli into a steamer basket; then cook for about 15 minutes or until broccoli is tender.

3.  In another saucepan, bring ¾ cup water to a boil. Slowly add the cornmeal, stirring constantly until it is dissolved. Reduce the heat and simmer for about 15 minutes, or according to the directions on the package.

4.  When the cornmeal is finished, drain the broccoli and mix it in with the cornmeal.

5.  Allow to cool, then fork-mash before serving.

### Yellow or White Cornmeal?

*For the purposes of making food for your baby, it doesn't really matter which type of cornmeal you choose. Yellow corn has a buttery taste, while white corn tends to be sweeter. Either way, your baby will get the nutrition he needs.*

# Baby's First Rice and Beans

*Rice and beans are a staple food in many parts of the world. They go together for a reason: beans provide a protein that's lacking in amino acids, but it's rounded out by serving it along with nuts or grains, like rice, to make a filling complete protein.*

●　●　●　●　●

**4 Servings**

*1 cup red beans*
*½ cup white rice*
*6 cups water*

1. Rinse the beans and place in a large saucepan along with 5 cups of water. Bring to a boil.

2. Reduce heat and simmer until beans are tender, about 2 hours.

3. In another saucepan, pour 1 cup of water and ½ cup of uncooked white rice. Bring to a boil; then reduce the heat and simmer for about 35 minutes, or according to the directions on the package.

4. When the beans are tender, drain and serve on top of the rice.

5. Allow to cool; then fork-mash before serving, or serve as finger food.

**2 Servings**

1 small white potato
½ cup Cheddar
1 tablespoon butter or
   margarine
2 cups of water

# Potato and Cheese

*While potato skins are loaded with fiber and are a great meal-maker, they're not so good for young babies. Skins are tough and don't mash easily with the gums, so if your little one is short on teeth, hold the skins for now.*

● ● ● ● ●

1. Wash and peel the potato. Dice into small pieces. Grate the cheese.

2. Bring 2 cups of water to a boil. Add the potato; then reduce heat and simmer for about 25 minutes, or until potato is completely tender.

3. Drain the water and return the potato to the saucepan. Add butter and cheese, stirring over low heat until the cheese is melted. Toss thoroughly.

4. Allow to cool; then fork-mash before serving.

### Is Butter Necessary?

*Most standard macaroni-and-cheese or potato-and-cheese recipes involve butter. Is all that fat really necessary? No, but a little bit of butter is helpful even in baby recipes. Without the fat from the butter, the cheese will melt and then immediately harden, leaving your baby with a difficult meal. Adding just a bit of butter to melting cheese helps keep it soft for longer.*

# Potato Pumpkin Mash

*Potatoes and pumpkins are a natural part of many fall meals. Cook this recipe up for the whole family! When serving to older children or adults, season appropriately with salt and pepper.*

*     *     *     *     *

1. Preheat the oven to 350°F. Slice the pumpkin in quarters, removing any seeds. Remove the skin, and dice the pumpkin flesh into small pieces.

2. Combine the potato and pumpkin in a saucepan with the water. Bring to a boil; then simmer for 30 minutes, or until the vegetables are tender.

3. Place the drained vegetables in an baking dish. Dot with butter and sprinkle the cheese on top.

4. Bake for 15 minutes, or until the cheese is melted. Let cool completely before serving.

### Cooking with Pumpkin
*Pumpkins are part of the same family as squashes, and both can be cooked and eaten. There are different varieties of pumpkins—the ones you carve on Halloween won't taste particularly good! Look for pumpkins called "cooking pumpkins," "pie pumpkins," or some other designation that indicates that they are meant to be eaten, not carved.*

### 3 Servings
1 small sweet potato or yam, diced
¼ small cooking pumpkin
1 tablespoon butter or margarine
½ cup shredded cheese
4 cups of water

# Steamed Tofu

**1 Serving**

*1 ounce tofu*
*2 tablespoons water*

*Tofu is a great food for your baby—it's soft, easy to mash, and high in protein. Bean curd is available in most grocery stores, and is a terrific finger food.*

* * * * *

1. Place tofu in a glass microwaveable dish, adding a little water in the bottom of the dish. Cover with microwave-safe plastic wrap.

2. Microwave on high for 30 seconds or until warm.

# Puréed Tofu with Fruit

**1 Serving**

*1 ounce silken tofu*
*1 large strawberry*

*When puréeing tofu, go for the soft silken variety of tofu. The firmer bean curds will purée, but may require a little additional liquid and won't be as smooth.*

* * * * *

1. Wash the strawberry and remove the stem.

2. Combine the tofu and the strawberry in a food processor or blender. Purée until smooth.

### Freeze That Leftover Tofu

*Freezing and thawing tofu tends to make it even more absorbent than it was originally! While adults may not like the soggier texture, it's great for babies who are learning to chew solids. Make a larger dish of tofu, and freeze the leftovers in ice-cube trays or small containers.*

# Fried Tofu Triangles

*If you're going to serve fried food to your baby, fried tofu is a pretty good choice. You don't need to deep-fry it; just brown it long enough to get a slightly crispy crust. Firmer tofu holds up better when flipping it over in the frying pan, so avoid the silken varieties for this recipe.*

* * * * *

1. Slice the tofu into small triangles.

2. Heat the oil in a large frying pan. Add the tofu and brown for 2–3 minutes.

3. Flip each piece over and brown for another 2–3 minutes.

4. When browned, drain the tofu onto clean paper towels. Let cool completely; then serve as finger food.

## Dipping Sauces

*Fried tofu is great when dipped in a mild sauce. Try mixing 2 tablespoons of soy sauce with a splash of rice vinegar. For a sweeter sauce, mix a tablespoon of peanut butter with a dash of soy sauce. To spice things up for older babies or adults, add a shake of garlic powder or red pepper.*

## 2 Servings

*2 ounces firm tofu*
*2 tablespoons oil*

**2 Servings**

2 ounces firm tofu
1 small carrot
2 large broccoli florets
½ small zucchini
2 tablespoons oil
1 cup chicken stock or water
1 teaspoon soy sauce
⅛ teaspoon ginger, ground
⅛ teaspoon garlic powder

# Stir-Fried Tofu with Vegetables

*When making Asian-style meals for your baby, go easy on the soy sauce because it's high in sodium. If possible, use the low-sodium variety. Also, especially when cooking with soy sauce, only use fresh chicken stock; avoid bouillon-based broth, because that is also loaded with sodium.*

＊　＊　＊　＊　＊

1. Wash the vegetables well. Peel the carrot, then dice all vegetables into small pieces.

2. Cut the tofu into small strips.

3. Heat the oil in a large frying pan. Add the tofu and stir-fry until brown, about 5 minutes.

4. Add vegetables, soy, garlic, ginger, and stock. Bring the stock to a boil; then stir-fry until all vegetables are cooked and tender, about 12–15 minutes.

5. Allow to cool; then fork-mash before serving if desired.

# Yogurt with Salmon

*Yogurt is a great addition to this recipe and makes the salmon a more palatable texture for young babies. But make sure to let the salmon cool first, and don't cook with the yogurt; too much heat will cause the yogurt to curdle.*

● ● ● ● ●

**2 Servings**

*1 thin salmon fillet*
*2 tablespoons water*
*½ cup plain yogurt*
*⅛ teaspoon dill*

1. Wash the salmon well, removing all bones. Place in the bottom of a microwaveable dish and sprinkle with dill.

2. Pour water into the bottom of the dish and cover with either a lid or microwave-safe plastic wrap.

3. Cook on high for 3 minutes. Let rest; then cook for another 3–4 minutes. Fish is done when it flakes easily with a fork and is an opaque color.

4. Once cooled, fork-mash the salmon and yogurt together.

## Go Wild

*Farm-raised salmon can contain more of contaminants such as PCBs (polychlorinated biphenyls) and dioxin than wild salmon. Also, farmed salmon tends to be higher in saturated fats because the fish exercise less. However, wild salmon may be more expensive, so choose wisely and vary the types of fish you serve.*

**2 Servings**

*1 small whitefish fillet*
*¼ cup water*

# Puréed Whitefish

*A simple high-protein meal, puréed fish goes great with puréed vegetable meals. It's also an easy recipe to make from leftovers! When you're cooking for the rest of the family, omit the heavy seasonings from one fillet, and you'll be all set to make your baby's meal.*

● ● ● ● ●

1. Wash the fish fillet, removing all bones.

2. Pour water into the bottom of a microwave-safe dish and cover with either a lid or microwave-safe plastic wrap.

3. Cook on high for 3 minutes. Let rest; then cook for another 3–4 minutes. Fish is done when it flakes easily with a fork and is an opaque color.

4. When cool, put fish into a food processor or blender. Purée for 30 seconds.

5. Add breastmilk or formula as needed, 1 tablespoon at a time, to make the mixture creamier.

### Allergy Alert

*If your child is prone to asthma or allergies, experts recommend holding off on seafood until your baby is 3 years old. Seafood is a common allergen, along with nuts, wheat, and dairy products. In particular, shellfish allergies can be quite severe. If your baby has shown no sign of allergies (or eczema) and other family members are not allergic, fish is safe to introduce after her first year, but hold off until later on foods like shrimp and crab.*

# Baby's Fish and Vegetables

*Oven-baked fish is a healthy meal for your baby, and can be a time-saver as well. Prepare this meal, pop it in the oven and, an hour later, dinner is served! Veggies will bake faster when sliced thinly, so go for thin coins rather than chunks in this recipe.*

●　●　●　●　●

1. Preheat the oven to 375°F. Wash and peel the carrot. Wash the zucchini, then cut both into thin slices.

2. Wash the fish fillet, removing all bones.

3. Prepare a double-layer of aluminum foil about 18-inch-square, and lightly grease the inside of the foil.

4. Place the fish and vegetables in the foil, dot the top with butter and lemon juice, then seal the packet and place in a baking dish. Bake for 45 minutes, or until the fish is opaque and flakes easily.

5. Allow to cool; then fork-mash before serving.

**3 Servings**

*1 small whitefish fillet*
*½ small zucchini*
*½ medium carrot*
*⅛ teaspoon lemon juice*
*½ tablespoon butter*

**2 Servings**

¼ cup cottage cheese
¼ cup cream cheese
¼ cup shredded Mozzarella
2 tablespoons milk

# Cheesy Delight

*Looking for a way to combine your baby's favorite cheeses into one recipe? Look no farther! As long as your baby has tolerated these different cheeses individually, try combining them into one delicious meal that will make for terrific leftovers.*

●　●　●　●　●

1. Put the cottage cheese into a medium bowl. Mash with a fork to remove the lumps.

2. Allow the cream cheese to warm to room temperature; then mix it into the cottage cheese with a spoon.

3. Stir in the Mozzarella, adding milk as needed to thin the mixture.

4. Either serve to baby as is, or fork-mash again before serving. Refrigerate the leftovers immediately.

### Serve It on Toast
*While some babies like to eat cheesy blends right from a spoon, others prefer it spread on toast or crackers. Try toasting a thick slice of whole-wheat bread, cutting into 1-inch strips, and serving to baby with a cheese spread on top. While he may just lick the cheese off, he may end up eating some wholesome grains as well!*

# Bacon Blend

**1 Serving**

*1 strip bacon*
*¼ cup cottage cheese*

*There's usually at least one leftover strip of bacon, so why not make it into a meal that your baby can enjoy as well? Serve in moderation, because bacon (while sinfully tasty) isn't one of the healthiest foods out there. If the fat content is a major concern, try using turkey bacon instead of pork.*

* * * * *

1. Place the bacon strip in a frying pan. Cook over medium-high heat. Flip after 2–3 minutes. Flip again after another 2–3 minutes. Watch carefully to make sure the bacon doesn't burn.

2. Alternatively, place the bacon on a paper towel on a microwave-safe plate. Cover with another paper towel and cook for about 2 minutes on high. Check every 30 seconds for doneness.

3. Drain the bacon and crumble into tiny pieces.

4. Put the cottage cheese into a medium bowl. Mash with a fork to remove the lumps. Add the bacon and continue fork-mashing to desired consistency.

5. If the mixture is too thick, add a tablespoon of water, breastmilk, or formula to thin.

## 2 Servings

¼ cup ground pork (about
    1–2 ounces)
¼ cup pineapple
¼ cup green pepper, diced
1 cup water

# Hawaiian Poached Pork

*Ground pork can be cooked in any number of ways, but poaching is a good method when making meals for your baby. Poaching keeps the moisture sealed in the meat, meaning your baby will have an easier time mashing it with her gums. Alternatives include pan-frying and oven-baking.*

●　●　●　●　●

1.  Cut up the pineapple into small chunks.

2.  Bring the water to a boil in a medium saucepan. Add pork. Simmer for 15–20 minutes or until pork is completely cooked.

3.  Drain pork and return to saucepan. Add pineapple and green pepper, and continue simmering for 10 minutes, or until vegetables are heated through and soft.

4.  Allow to cool; then fork-mash or purée before serving.

### Canned Is Okay

*If fresh pineapples aren't available, canned pineapple is perfectly acceptable for this recipe. As long as you get the variety that's not made with heavy syrup, canned pineapple may even be preferable because you can also use the juice instead of water to provide additional flavor to the pork while it's cooking.*

# Simple Whitefish

*Whitefish is easily digested and has a mild flavor, so it's a terrific new food to incorporate into your baby's diet. Cod, haddock, perch, tilapia, and orange roughy are readily available and provide your baby with plenty of nutrients, including protein.*

* * * * *

1. Wash the fish fillet, remove all bones, and sprinkle lightly with salt.

2. Dredge the fillet in flour. Shake to remove any excess.

3. Heat the oil in a frying pan. Fry the fillet until brown, 4–5 minutes.

4. Flip and cook on the other side 4–5 minutes, or until fish is cooked through and flakes with a fork.

5. Allow to cool; then fork-mash before serving.

**2 Servings**

*1 small white fish fillet
1 tablespoon olive oil
¼ cup all-purpose flour
dash salt*

# Potato and Chicken Stew

*Another versatile dish, this tasty meal combines chicken with potatoes and cheese. You can also use leftover cooked chicken or potato in this recipe.*

* * * * *

1. Bring 2 cups water to a boil in a medium saucepan. Add the chicken, reduce to a simmer, and cook for about 20 minutes, or until chicken is completely cooked.

2. In a separate saucepan, bring 2 cups of water to a boil. Add the potato; then cook for 20–25 minutes, or until potato is soft.

3. Drain the chicken, dice into small pieces, and return to the saucepan. Add in the potato and milk; then simmer for about 10 minutes.

4. Add the cheese to the saucepan and stir until the cheese is melted. Allow to cool; then fork-mash or purée before serving.

**3 Servings**

*1 half chicken breast (about
    4 ounces)
1 small white potato, peeled
    and diced
¼ cup milk (regular or soy)
¼ cup shredded cheese
4 cups water*

## 2 Servings

¼ cup ground beef (about 2
    ounces)
½ cup green beans
2 cup water
3 tablespoons all-purpose
    flour
1 tablespoon butter
½ cup milk

# Ground Beef and Green Beans

*There are different types of ground beef, and they generally have different fat contents. Ground chuck tends to be the fattiest (15%–25% fat), and ground sirloin or ground round are lower in fat. The higher-fat meats will be more tender, so they may be a better choice for baby.*

* * * * *

1.  Brown the ground beef in a frying pan for 10–15 minutes, or until completely cooked. Drain on paper towels.

2.  Wash and trim the beans. Place in a steamer basket inside a saucepan with 2 cups of water. Bring to a boil; then simmer for 15 minutes, or until beans are completely tender. Or, use frozen green beans and shorten the cooking time to 8–10 minutes.

3.  In a small saucepan, melt the butter over low heat. Stir in the flour, whisking constantly until dissolved. Add milk, stirring constantly, until it thickens into a white sauce.

4.  Combine the beans and beef in the frying pan. Pour in the white sauce and simmer over low heat until it is completely mixed in.

5.  Allow to cool, then fork-mash or purée before serving. The ground beef will give this meal some texture, so it's great for older babies.

## Buying Ground Beef

*Ground beef turns red when exposed to oxygen (in the packaging plant, usually). Red beef is fresh and safe to eat. If you notice the beef appears to be turning brown or gray, stay away—it's probably starting to spoil. Since grinding beef exposes more of the meat's surface to air, it spoils faster than unground cuts.*

# Fish Chowder with Corn

*Chowder is a type of thick, creamy soup that usually contains seafood and/or potatoes. The starch from the potatoes binds the soup into a stew, and the resulting smooth texture is great for young eaters. If fork-mashing leaves too many discrete pieces, purée in the food processor before serving.*

* * * * *

**2 Servings**

*1 small whitefish fillet*
*⅛ cup corn*
*⅛ cup peas*
*½ medium white potato, diced*
*1 tablespoon butter*
*¼ cup milk (regular or soy)*
*2 cups water*

1. Combine potato, corn, and peas in a saucepan with 2 cups of water. Bring to a boil; then cook for 25 minutes, or until the potatoes are soft.

2. Wash the fish fillet, removing all bones. Place fish into the bottom of a microwave-safe dish and add enough water to cover the bottom of the dish. Cover with either a lid or microwave-safe plastic wrap.

3. Cook fish in the microwave on high for 3 minutes. Let rest; then cook for another 3–4 minutes. Fish is done when it flakes easily with a fork and is an opaque color.

4. Drain the vegetables. Add the fish, butter, and milk, stirring over low heat until the chowder thickens. Allow to cool; then fork-mash or purée before serving.

## The Origins of Chowder

*According to most sources, the soup we know as chowder originated in England in the 1700s. Fishermen would start a pot of water boiling in the morning and, as the day wore on, would add fresh fish, vegetables, bread, and any other available ingredients. By day's end, a thick soup was ready for all.*

## 3 Servings

1 half chicken breast (about 4 ounces)
1 small apple
½ orange
2 tablespoons apple juice
2 tablespoons orange juice

## 2 Servings

¼ cup ground beef (about 1–2 ounces)
½ cup noodles
½ cup shredded cheese
3 cups water

# Fruity Chicken Casserole

*Many "grown-up" chicken casseroles are made with heavy cream and canned soups. For young babies, it's best to know exactly what you're cooking with, down to the last ingredient. Try this lighter, fruity variation on the chicken casserole instead.*

•　•　•　•　•

1. Preheat the oven to 350°F. Wash and peel the apple. Remove the core and seeds; then dice the fruit into small pieces. Place in a greased baking dish.

2. Wash the chicken breast; then place on top of the fruit.

3. Mix the orange and apple juice together and pour over the chicken.

4. Bake for 45 minutes, or until chicken juices run clear.

5. Allow to cool; then fork-mash or purée before serving.

# Beef Noodle Dinner

*Wide egg noodles go very well with ground beef, and this is a good meal for self-feeding. The flat shape of the noodles makes it easy for babies to pick up, and fewer noodles will go sliding onto the floor. You can also substitute curly pasta or bowties.*

•　•　•　•　•

1. Brown the ground beef in a frying pan for 8–10 minutes, or until completely cooked. Drain on paper towels.

2. Boil the water in a medium saucepan. Add the noodles and cook for 20 minutes, or until the noodles are completely tender.

3. Drain the pasta; then combine it and the beef in the saucepan. Over low heat, add the cheese and stir until melted.

4. Allow to cool; then allow your baby to self-feed under supervision.

# Beef Stew

*Homemade beef stew is a terrific meal for a cold winter's day. The long cooking time tenderizes the beef, making it a good choice for your teething baby. Stew meat is tougher than other types of beef, so it's not a good choice for quicker cooking preparations.*

• • • • •

## 3 Servings

4 ounces stew beef, cubed
1 tablespoon oil
3 tablespoons all-purpose
   flour
2 cups beef stock or water
½ small onion
1 medium carrot
½ cups milk

1. Shake 1 tablespoon of flour and beef together in a plastic bag, coating the beef. Heat the oil in a frying pan; then brown the beef for 3–4 minutes per side.

2. Add the broth and reduce heat to a simmer. Cook for 45 minutes.

3. Wash and peel the carrot and onion. Dice both into small pieces. Put into the stew pot and cook for another hour.

4. In a small bowl, mix 1 tablespoon of flour with about ¼ cup of water. Mix thoroughly; then stir into the stew pot along with the milk. Stir the stew until it starts to thicken. Cook for another 10 minutes.

5. Allow to cool; then fork-mash or purée before serving.

### Fork-Mashing Beef

*Stew meat gets very tender when cooked, but even so, it may be too chewy for infants to handle. If you don't want to completely purée it, try using a ricer (or potato masher) instead of a fork. Also, adding liquid when mashing will make the mixture softer and easier to chew.*

**3 Servings**

½ boneless, skinless chicken
breast (about 4 ounces),
diced
1 tablespoon mild red curry
paste
1 teaspoon oil
½ cup coconut milk
1 small white potato, diced
1 cup chicken stock or water

# Mild Chicken and Coconut Curry Purée

*This curry dish will go nicely with white or brown rice; simply
serve the curry on top of the rice and fork-mash together.*

●　●　●　●　●

1. Cook the curry paste and oil in a medium saucepan for 2–3 minutes,
   watching carefully to make sure it doesn't burn.

2. Add chicken to curry and brown the chicken for 3–4 minutes.

3. Add potato, coconut milk, and chicken stock to the saucepan.

4. Simmer for 25–30 minutes, or until the potato and chicken are cooked
   through. Stir occasionally to prevent sticking.

5. Allow to cool; then fork-mash before serving.

### A Splash of Green
*Cooking yellow or red curry for your baby? If you serve the same dish
to older children or grownups, try adding a little green with a sprig of
parsley, or garnish the dish with steamed broccoli florets. The colors
and tastes will provide a nice contrast to the coconut-flavored curry.*

# Tomato and Mushroom Pasta

**2 Servings**

½ cup pasta
1 teaspoon oil
¼ cup white button
  mushrooms
1 medium fresh tomato
⅛ teaspoon basil
2 cups water

*There are literally hundreds of types of tomatoes that you can grow in your backyard. Home-grown tomatoes are great for your baby, of course, but tomato vines can rapidly take over a small garden. Cherry or pear tomatoes are great for snacking, while the larger beefsteak tomatoes will produce plenty of tender fruit for meals.*

●　●　●　●　●

1. Bring the water to a boil in a medium saucepan. Add the pasta, then cook for 10–15 minutes, or until pasta is very tender.

2. Heat the oil in a small frying pan. Sauté the mushrooms for 6–7 minutes, or until tender.

3. Wash and dice the tomato, removing the stem and any tough white parts. Add to the frying pan with basil and sauté for 15–18 minutes, or until very tender.

4. Drain pasta and toss with the mushroom-tomato mix.

5. Allow to cool; then fork-mash before serving.

## 2 Servings

½ boneless, skinless chicken
    breast (about 4 ounces),
    diced
¼ cup white or brown rice
½ tablespoon butter
1 cup chicken stock or water

# Chicken and Rice

*Chicken and rice is a very flexible dish; it can be made in any number of ways, with an array of different seasonings and spices. This variety is oven-baked for convenience; one-dish meals are quick to prepare and clean up, giving you more time with your baby, and less time slaving away in the kitchen.*

·  ·  ·  ·  ·

1. Grease a small baking dish. Pour the stock and rice into the bottom and mix to distribute the rice evenly. Dot the top with butter.

2. Place chicken on top of the rice.

3. Cover the dish with a lid or foil and bake at 350°F for 1 hour, or until the chicken juices run clear when pricked with a fork.

4. Allow to cool; then purée in a food processor or blender before serving.

### Cook It in Bulk

*You can save money by making the entire family's dinner in one pan. This results in less time to keep the oven on, fewer dishes to wash, and fewer trips to the store. Just quadruple the recipe, and you'll have enough for several adults and your baby. Pair with a green vegetable like steamed broccoli or a green salad, and dinner's done!*

# Banana-Grape Yogurt Dessert

**1 Serving**

½ banana
¼ cup seedless grapes
¼ cup yogurt

*While grapes are a choking hazard for the under-one crowd, older babies can start eating grapes as long as they are sliced into halves or quarters. Let your baby self-feed these sorts of fruits, so she can regulate how much she puts in her mouth at a time. As always, supervise!*

•  •  •  •  •

1.  Peel the banana, removing any brown spots, and cut into thin coins.

2.  Wash the grapes and slice into quarters.

3.  Combine in a bowl with yogurt in top.

4.  Let your baby self-feed under careful supervision.

**8 Servings**

3 cups flour
1 ½ cups sugar
½ teaspoon salt
1 teaspoon vanilla extract
¾ cup butter or margarine,
    softened
1 tablespoon baking powder
5 egg yolks

# Baby's First Birthday Cake

*There are few things more memorable in parents' lives than their child's first birthday. Make it special by cooking up a homemade cake to celebrate. This recipe is a classic triple-layer yellow cake, made with egg yolks instead of whole eggs.*

•   •   •   •   •

1.  Preheat the oven to 350°F. Grease three 8-inch round cake pans, line the bottoms with waxed paper, and grease and flour the pans.

2.  Cream the butter with 1 cup of sugar. When mixed, add flour, salt and baking powder.

3.  Beat in egg yolks, one at a time. Add vanilla and last ½ cup sugar.

4.  Fill each cake pan about halfway; then bake for 20–25 minutes or until a toothpick inserted into the center comes out clean.

5.  Cool in the pans for about 10 minutes; then remove onto wire racks and let the cakes cool completely.

### Quick Cake Frosting

*For a triple layer cake, beat ½ cup butter with an electric mixer. Once the butter is fluffy, gradually add 3 cups of confectioners' sugar and 3 tablespoons of milk or water. Continue mixing until the frosting is a spreadable consistency. If it's too runny, add more sugar; if it's too stiff to spread, just add more liquid.*

# First Rice Pudding

*Looking for a way to use up that leftover rice? Rice pudding is an excellent choice. This method yields a boiled rice pudding, which involves making your own rice; if you have leftover rice, place it and the other ingredients in a baking dish, and bake at 350°F for 45 minutes.*

* * * * *

**3 Servings**

½ cup white rice
1¼ cup milk (regular or soy)
2 teaspoons white or brown sugar
¼ teaspoon vanilla extract

1. Bring 1 cup of milk and rice to a scalding point (watch carefully so the milk doesn't boil).

2. Reduce to a simmer; then cook for 30 minutes, or according to package directions. Rice is done when the liquid is absorbed and rice is fluffy.

3. Give the rice a good stir. Add sugar, vanilla, and ¼ cup milk.

4. Simmer over low heat for about 10 minutes, or until the liquid is mostly absorbed.

5. Allow to cool; then fork-mash or purée before serving.

*4 slices bread*
*1 egg*
*½ cup evaporated milk*
*1 tablespoon melted butter*
*3 tablespoons brown sugar*
*½ teaspoon vanilla extract*
*¼ teaspoon cinnamon*

# Bread Pudding

*Bread pudding is of British origin, but it's very popular in some parts of the United States as well. It's one of the best uses for leftover bread, and it doesn't matter how stale the bread is—baking in eggs and sugar will soften it right up. Bread pudding has a nice, soft texture that's easy for your baby to handle.*

* * * * *

1. Preheat the oven to 350°F.

2. Cut the bread into cubes and place in the bottom of a greased oven-proof baking dish.

3. Mix the egg, evaporated milk, butter, sugar, vanilla, and cinnamon into a bowl. Pour over the bread cubes and let it soak for 10–15 minutes.

4. Bake for 45 minutes, or until a toothpick inserted into the center comes out clean.

5. Allow to cool; then fork-mash before serving.

### Variations

*When making bread pudding for grownups, it's traditional to serve it with a sauce on top. While some tame versions involve a caramel sauce, many use a whiskey or bourbon sauce. If you're making a larger batch of pudding for the family, be sure to add these toppings after your baby has had his share!*

# Baby's Apple Pie

*Apple pie for baby is just like apple pie for grownups—except without the pie shell! Babies don't need all the shortening or butter in a typical pie crust, and it will often be too chewy for easy gumming. Try this recipe instead, because it'll give your baby all of the flavors of homemade apple pie.*

• • • • •

**2 Servings**

1 red apple
1 teaspoon brown sugar
⅛ teaspoon lemon juice
⅛ teaspoon cinnamon
⅛ cup rice powder
2 cups water

1. Wash, peel, and core the apple. Chop into small chunks.

2. Put apple pieces in a small saucepan with 1½ cups of water, lemon juice, sugar, and cinnamon. Bring to a boil; then simmer for 25 minutes, or until apple is very soft. Stir occasionally.

3. In another small saucepan, bring ½ cup of water to a boil. Add the rice powder and stir for 30 seconds. Cover the pot, turn down the heat to low, and simmer for 7–8 minutes, or until the rice is a smooth, thick consistency. Stir occasionally to prevent sticking.

4. When the apple is cooked, fork-mash. Mix in the cooked rice cereal until it reaches the desired consistency.

*1 fresh peach*
*1 teaspoon brown sugar*
*⅛ teaspoon cinnamon*
*⅛ cup rice powder*
*2 cups water*

# Baby's Peach Cobbler

*Traditional peach cobbler is a baked fruit dish with a sweet biscuit top-*
*ping. Because most babies wouldn't be able to eat the topping once it's*
*baked and hard, here's a variation on an old favorite, and one that's*
*tailored right to your baby's developing abilities.*

⁕ ⁕ ⁕ ⁕ ⁕

1. Preheat oven to 350°F.

2. Wash the peach and cut into thin slices. Remove the skin.

3. Place peach into a small greased baking dish with brown sugar and cin-namon. Give it a quick stir; then bake for 30 minutes, or until peaches are completely soft.

4. In a small saucepan, bring ½ cup of water to a boil. Add the rice powder and stir for 30 seconds. Cover the pot, turn down the heat to low, and simmer for 7–8 minutes, or until the rice is a smooth, thick consistency. Stir occasionally to prevent sticking.

5. When the peach is cooked, fork-mash. Mix in the cooked rice cereal until the cobbler reaches the desired consistency.

### Cobbling Together a Dessert

*Cobblers are fruit desserts that are traditionally cooked in deep-dish*
*pans. They're historically made with whatever fruits are in season;*
*blueberry, blackberry, apricot, and apple are all popular cobbler fla-*
*vors. Cobblers are distinguished from other baked fruit desserts*
*because they're usually topped with a sweet biscuit dough.*

# Pears and Peaches

*Looking for a fruit dessert with no added starches? Look no farther! This recipe uses summer fruits with simple seasonings. Canned fruits also work well here, as long as you use the varieties that are not made with heavy syrup.*

* * * * *

1. Preheat the oven to 350°F.

2. Wash the pear and peach. Remove the cores and skin, then dice into small pieces.

3. Combine into a small greased baking dish along with sugars, vanilla, and cinnamon. Give it a quick stir; then bake for about 30 minutes, or until the fruit is completely soft.

4. When the fruit is cooked, fork-mash or purée to the desired consistency.

**3 Servings**

1 peach
1 fresh pear
⅛ teaspoon cinnamon
⅛ teaspoon brown sugar
1 teaspoon white sugar
⅛ teaspoon vanilla extract

# Pear Dessert

*For a grown-up variation, mix the butter and sugar and pour them on top of the fruit before baking, to form a sweet crispy shell.*

* * * * *

1. Peel and core the pear. Dice into small pieces and mix with butter, cinnamon, and sugar.

2. Bake in a baking dish at 350°F for 30 minutes.

3. When the pear is cooked, fork-mash or purée to the desired consistency.

**1 Serving**

1 pear
⅛ teaspoon cinnamon
2 teaspoons brown sugar
2 teaspoons melted butter

## Baked Apples

**1 Serving**

1 apple
1 teaspoon white sugar
⅛ teaspoon cinnamon
¼ cup water

*For the older children, make a caramel sauce from butter and brown sugar; then pour it inside the apple with raisins or cinnamon candies. Serve with ice cream.*

•  •  •  •  •

1.  Preheat the oven to 350°F. Wash the apple. Remove the top core, leaving the apple intact.

2.  Sprinkle sugar and cinnamon on the inside of the apple. Pour the water into a small baking dish, then place the apple in the center. Bake for about 45 minutes, or until the apple is completely cooked.

3.  When cooled, fork-mash to a suitable consistency. If desired, the entire skin can be removed once the apple is cooked.

### Make a Dumpling Out of It

*A fun trick for toddlers or older children is, instead of baked fruit, to make baked fruit dumplings! Combine 1 cup flour, ½ cup shortening, 2 tablespoons ice water, and a dash of salt to make a dough. Knead for a couple of minutes; then wrap around your fruit and seal with a tight pinch. Bake at a slightly higher temperature, around 400°F.*

# 18–24 Months

**1 Serving**

*½ cup cottage cheese*
*½ peach*
*1 plum*
*1 apricot*

# Cottage Cheese with Fruit

*Summer fruit with cottage cheese is a great combination for young eaters. This simple meal provides protein along with healthy fruit. To make the dish a little soupier, slice the fruit on a saucer; pour any juice that comes out right on top of the cottage cheese.*

* * * * *

1. Wash and peel the peach, remove the pit, and cut into thin slices.

2. Wash the plum, remove the pit and cut into thin slices.

3. Wash and peel apricot, remove the pit, and cut into pieces.

4. Place a scoop of cottage cheese into a baby-safe dish. Spoon the fruit on top.

5. Fork-mash if desired.

### Beyond Purées
*Once your child is 18–24 months old, almost none of her food will need to be puréed. While she may still enjoy thinner textures, it's also a good idea to challenge her with more chewing foods. Most recipes for this age group can be fork-mashed or simply served as is.*

# Fresh Fruit Salad

*Fruit salad is one of the true joys of summer. And the best part: you can substitute any of the ingredients with whatever is in season. It's nice to provide a combination of flavors, colors, and textures; just make sure the pieces are the right size for your child to pick up with his fingers.*

• • • • • •

**3 Servings**

1 kiwi
¼ cup strawberries
¼ cup blueberries
¼ cup raspberries
½ small mango
½ cup seedless grapes

1. Wash the kiwi well and trim off both ends. Slide a tablespoon between the fleshy fruit and the peel. Run the spoon around the entire edge, and the fruit should slide out intact. Cut into small pieces.

2. Wash the berries and remove any stems. Cut the strawberries into quarters. Blueberries and raspberries can either be served whole or, if they're large, cut in half.

3. Remove skin and pit from mango. Slice into small pieces.

4. Wash the grapes and slice each in half.

5. Combine all fruits in a baby-safe bowl, and refrigerate until ready to use. Fork-mash if desired.

**2 Servings**

¼ cup shredded coconut
½ cup pineapple
½ cup mandarin oranges or
    tangerine
½ cup papaya

# Coconut and Fruit Salad

*This salad is a sweet and refreshing departure from regular fruitsalad for your toddler. Halved mandarin orange slices are the perfect size for your toddler to pick up.*

●　●　●　●　●

1.  Dice the pineapple into small chunks.

2.  If using canned mandarin oranges, slice each piece in half. If using fresh tangerine, peel and remove seeds, and then cut each piece in thirds.

3.  Slice the papaya in half and remove seeds and skin. Cut into small chunks.

4.  Combine the fruits in a baby-safe bowl and mix with the coconut. Refrigerate until ready to use. Fork-mash if desired.

### Mandarin Oranges

*The mandarin orange is about the size of a tangerine but usually has a redder skin. The clementine is a small, North Afican mandarin orange hybrid. Mandarins are native to Southeast Asia, but are also grown in the warm American Southwest.*

# Bread Crumb–Peach Pudding

**2 Servings**

1 cup all-purpose flour
½ cup brown sugar
1 egg
½ cup bread crumbs
1 peach
1 teaspoon light cane syrup
¼ teaspoon baking soda
¼ cup milk

*This type of boiled pudding is hundreds of years old, and originates in England. The "grown-up" version adds a fair amount of brandy before baking, but you will want to omit this in a recipe for the children. This is sometimes called Christmas pudding because it's typically made in the late fall, and then aged until the end of December.*

⬤　⬤　⬤　⬤　⬤

1. Peel the peach and remove the pit. Dice into small pieces.

2. Combine the flour, sugar, milk, peach, baking soda, and bread crumbs in a bowl. Mix well.

3. Add in the egg and cane syrup. Continue mixing until all ingredients are thoroughly combined.

4. Fill a large pot with several inches of water. Place a steaming rack inside the pot. Place on the stove and bring the water to a boil. Pour the recipe into a pudding steamer and cover. Cook for about 4 hours, or until the pudding is completely set.

## Steaming a Pudding

*Making an authentic steamed pudding is not an easy task, but it's a skill worth learning if it's something you plan to make on a regular basis. The main pieces of equipment you'll need are a large pot with a steaming rack and a pudding steamer. A pudding steamer is a metal vessel that will fit inside your steaming pot, and the pudding goes inside this pudding steamer (also called a pudding mold).*

1 small cantaloupe or
    honeydew melon
1 cup yogurt
½ cup blueberries

# Melon Bowls with Yogurt

*Just about any small melon can be used for this recipe, and it's a fun one for
small children to help prepare. Allow your child to scoop out the melon seeds with
a spoon or an ice-cream scoop, and encourage her to eat the yogurt directly from
the melon. Start her out on a road to healthy eating!*

● ● ● ● ●

1.  Slice the melon in half. Slice a small piece of shell off the bottom so that
    the melon will sit easily on a plate.

2.  Scoop out and discard all seeds.

3.  Wash the blueberries well, sort out any damaged berries. If using large
    berries, cut each in half.

4.  Fill the hollow in the melon with yogurt. Top with berries.

5.  If your baby has trouble scooping the melon out, assist by removing
    pieces using a melon baller or grapefruit spoon.

# Baked Zucchini

*Baking zucchini with tomato sauce and cheese is almost like giving your toddler pizza—but a healthier one that's also lower in fat. Add salt and pepper for older kids.*

**2 Servings**

*1 medium zucchini*
*½ cup tomato sauce*
*½ cup shredded Mozzarella*
*1 tablespoon oil*

• • • • •

1. Preheat the oven to 350°F. Scrub the zucchini and trim both ends. Slice into rings.

2. Place zucchini into a baking dish. Smother with tomato sauce and Mozzarella and oil, then cover the dish

3. Bake for 45 minutes, or until zucchini is very soft and cheese is melted. Serve as is or fork-mash if desired.

# Carrot Peels

**1 Serving**

*1 carrot*

*Carrots are loaded with vitamins A and E, and are great for babies. Carrot peels are soft enough to be gummed with fewer teeth, but have all the nutrition.*

• • • • •

1. Wash and peel the carrot. Trim off both ends.

2. Using a vegetable peeler, peel off thin strips of carrot. Serve as finger food.

½ cup cucumber
2 tablespoons sour cream
2 tablespoons mayonnaise
dash of salt
dash of dill

# Cucumbers and Dip

*Try different kinds of cucumber in addition to the traditional cucumbers
you'll find at the grocery store. English hothouse cucumbers and
Armenian cucumbers, for example, don't need to be peeled.*

●　●　●　●　●

1. Wash and peel the cucumber. Cut into thin slices.

2. Mix the sour cream, mayonnaise, salt, and dill. Serve as a dipping
   sauce for cucumber slices.

### Leftover Cucumber Ideas

*Try making a light Japanese salad out of leftover cucumber! Prepare a
sauce with ¼ cup rice vinegar, 1 tablespoon sugar, and a dash of salt.
Slice the leftover cucumber into thin rings; then place in a dish and
pour the sauce on top. It's best served chilled. Be sure to offer your
toddler a taste; some children actually like the pungent vinegar.*

# Bell Pepper Faces

*Here's a fun way to encourage your toddler to eat vegetables. Go for contrasting colors; reds, greens, and oranges will stand out nicely against a white or yellow tortilla. It doesn't matter if your baby's meal looks like a Rembrandt painting, but he'll be more excited about it if it's colorful.*

• • • • •

1. Place the tortilla on a flat plate. Slice the cherry tomato in half. Place on the tortilla for eyes.

2. Slice the bell pepper in half and remove all seeds. Cut 5–10 thin strips; place at the top of the tortilla for hair.

3. Cut the cheese into 2 half-circles. Place at the sides of the tortilla for ears.

4. Wash and peel the carrot. Grate several pieces and place on the tortilla for the mouth and eyebrows.

5. When the vegetables are all positioned the way you like them, affix each to the tortilla with a dab of peanut butter.

## Peppers

*Red, green, or yellow bell peppers are sweet and crunchy. Their hotter cousins, such as the jalapeño or the cayenne, will bring tears to your eyes and do much worse for a toddler. Hot peppers contain capsaicin, an alkaloid that forms the basis of pepper sprays. Good for people who thrive on spicy food, but keep it out of your toddler's meal.*

### 1 Serving

*¼ green pepper*
*1 cherry tomato*
*1 slice cheese*
*1 flour or corn tortilla*
*½ carrot*
*1 tablespoon peanut butter*

½ cup sugar snap-pea pods
2 cups water
2 teaspoons butter
⅛ teaspoon oregano
⅛ teaspoon parsley

# Pea Pods

*Shelling peas is an arduous process that requires some amount of patience. Freshly shelled peas, though, are well worth the effort! Sugar-snap peas can be eaten right in the shells. A toddler can eat peas whole or open them up after they're cooked, picking out the tender peas herself.*

* * * * *

1. If using fresh pea pods, select ones that are firm, bright-green, and medium-sized. Snap the ends off, and remove the strings from each pea.

2. Bring the water to a boil. Add the peas, then boil for about 8 minutes, or until the shells are tender.

3. Cut each cooked pea pod in half.

4. Either serve as is, or prepare a butter herb sauce by melting the butter in a small saucepan and stirring in the herbs. When thoroughly mixed, toss with the peas.

### Veggie Dips

*Vegetables can be dipped into just about any sauce your child might like. Try an Asian dipping sauce with 2 tablespoons soy sauce and ⅛ teaspoon sesame oil. Add a dash of pepper, garlic powder, and sugar. Or offer a mustard dip: 1 tablespoon mayonnaise, 1 tablespoon sour cream, and 1 teaspoon of mustard.*

# Parmesan Butter Noodles

*Parmesan is an aged cheese that has a stronger flavor than some of the milder cheeses, such as Monterey jack or American. You can either grate Parmesan yourself from a block of cheese, or purchase it grated. Either way, leftover grated cheese should be refrigerated to maintain freshness.*

• • • • •

1. Bring the water to a rapid boil in a large saucepan.

2. While the water is boiling, grate about a tablespoon of Parmesan cheese (or substitute grated cheese).

3. Add pasta and stir to separate the noodles. Continue boiling for 10–12 minutes, or according to package directions. Pasta should be soft and completely cooked.

4. Drain the pasta and return to the pot, cooking over very low heat. Add the butter and parmesan; toss until completely melted.

5. Serve as finger food, or fork-mash if desired.

### Spice It Up!
*Feel free to enhance the flavors of a simple butter-pasta recipe with additional cheeses or spices. Try adding a dash of pepper and granulated garlic, for example, and stir in with the butter. Need a little color in this mostly yellow dish? Add a dash of paprika—it's fairly mild-flavored and adds a fun reddish tint.*

**1 Serving**

*¼ cup egg noodles*
*4 cups of water*
*½ tablespoon butter or margarine*
*1 tablespoon Parmesan*

## Pasta with Carrot Peels

**1 Serving**

¼ cup egg noodles
4 cups of water
½ tablespoon butter or
    margarine
½ carrot

*A fun variation on this recipe is Rolled Pasta! Instead of egg noodles or spaghetti, boil 1–2 long lasagna noodles. When cooked, spread a bit of cream cheese on one side of a noodle. Then place carrot peels on the inside, and simply roll it up. Slice into 1-inch pieces, and serve as finger food.*

· · · · ·

1. Bring the water to a rapid boil in a large saucepan.

2. While the water is boiling, wash and peel the carrot. Trim off both ends. Using a vegetable peeler, peel off strips of carrot and set aside.

3. Add pasta to the boiling water and stir to separate the noodles. Continue boiling for 10–12 minutes, or according to package directions. Pasta should be soft and completely cooked.

4. Drain the pasta and return to the pot, cooking over very low heat. Add the butter and carrots. Stir until the butter is melted; then toss to coat the pasta and carrots.

5. Serve as finger food, or fork-mash if desired.

# Tomato Pasta

*Combine the freshness of garden-ripe tomatoes with the nourishing goodness of pasta! This recipe can be as light or rich as you choose. Using milk in the sauce will create a lighter summer meal, while you could instead substitute heavy cream for a richer, denser pasta.*

● ● ● ● ●

1. Bring the water to a boil in a medium saucepan. Add the pasta, then cook for 10–15 minutes, or until pasta is very tender.

2. Drain the pasta and return to the pot, cooking over very low heat. Add the butter and dill, tossing to coat the pasta.

3. In a small bowl, rapidly whisk the flour and milk together. When the flour is completely mixed in, slowly pour the mixture into the pasta.

4. Continue stirring the pasta until the sauce thickens.

5. Wash the cherry tomatoes and slice in half. Combine with the pasta and stir gently to mix.

### Trade for Veggies

*Save money on vegetables by setting up a vegetable exchange in your neighborhood. Most people with tomato or zucchini plants will usually be overrun with fresh produce during the high season. Plan to trade a bucket of apples from your tree, for example, for a box of fresh garden tomatoes.*

**1 Serving**

½ cup uncooked pasta
4 cups water
½ tablespoon butter or
    margarine
¼ cup cherry tomatoes
⅛ teaspoon dill
1 tablespoon all-purpose
    flour
½ cup milk (regular or soy)

1 cup fresh leafy greens
2 cups water
2 tablespoons sliced
   almonds
2 tablespoon butter or
   margarine

# Leafy Greens with Almonds

*This is a fun recipe that uses lots of spinach. Leafy green vegetables are some of the most beneficial ones out there. Most toddlers need little encouragement if they've been offered such vegetables from a young age. Almonds add a pleasant crunch, but don't substitute walnuts or peanuts; those nuts are larger and chunkier, and not safe for young children.*

●　●　●　●　●

1. Wash the green leaves thoroughly, removing any damaged parts.

2. Steam in a small amount of water for about 10 minutes, or until the vegetables turn a bright green color.

3. Melt the butter in a small frying pan. Toast the almonds for about 5 minutes, stirring constantly to prevent burning.

4. When the almonds are toasted, mix with the spinach. Fork-mash if desired.

# Best Baked Potatoes

**2 Servings**

1 medium russet potato
½ tablespoon oil

*If you don't have an hour to bake a potato in the oven, don't despair. They can also be cooked in the microwave with little sacrifice in flavor. Follow the same washing and pricking instructions; then cook on high for 5 minutes. Turn the potato over and cook for another 4–5 minutes. If the potato middle isn't soft, cook for another 1-2 minutes and recheck.*

● ● ● ● ●

1. Preheat the oven to 350°F.

2. Scrub the potato thoroughly with a vegetable brush. Cut out any bad spots.

3. Pat the potato dry with a paper towel; then poke 8–10 holes into the potato, using a fork or other sharp implement.

4. Pour the oil into a paper towel and rub it around the potato. Place on a baking sheet and bake for 1 hour, or until the potato skin is crispy.

5. When cooled, cut the potato in half. Scoop out the potato from the skin, and fork-mash if desired.

### Good Potatoes for Baking
*The russet is the quintessential type of potato used for making baked potatoes and potato skins. There are several types of russet potatoes: Burbank, Norgold, Frontier, and Ranger are just a few varieties. Yellow and red potatoes also bake well, though with their thinner skins, they may fare better in the microwave.*

*1 medium sweet potato
or yam*

# Baked Sweet Potatoes

*There is a variety of different kinds of sweet potatoes. Yams have a bright orange
interior and a sweet taste and soft texture. True sweet potatoes are lighter and firmer.*

•  •  •  •  •

1.  Scrub the sweet potato thoroughly with a vegetable brush. Cut out any bad spots. Poke 8–10 holes into the potato, using a fork or other sharp implement.

2.  Bake at 350°F for 1 hour, or until the potato skin is crispy.

3.  When cooled, cut the potato in half. Scoop out the potato from the skin, and fork-mash if desired.

**Too Dry**

*If your baked potatoes come out too dry, it's probably due to a combi-
nation of factors, starting with temperature. Cooking potatoes at
400°F makes the outside cook faster than the inside, leaving you with
a burned skin and a hard, dry, undercooked middle. Also, look at the
type of potato; yellow-fleshed potatoes tend to be dryer than their
white-fleshed cousins.*

# Green Beans and Potatoes

*Potatoes and beans are a nice colorful dish. Toddlers will be drawn to the bright greens and whites, which may be a pleasant change from the monotone purées she used to get! If you're inspired, add some cooked red bell peppers to this mix for an even brighter combination of vegetables.*

● ● ● ● ●

**1 Serving**

*1 small new potato*
*½ cup green beans*
*2 cups chicken stock or water*

1. Scrub the potato thoroughly with a vegetable brush. Cut out any bad spots; then dice into small pieces.

2. Wash the beans and snap off the ends. Cut into 1-inch segments.

3. Bring the chicken stock to boiling in a medium saucepan. Add the potatoes and cook for 15 minutes.

4. Add in the green beans and cook for another 8–10 minutes. If bright-green beans are too firm for baby, cook another 4–5 minutes; they will lose some of their color, but will be easier for toddlers to mash with their gums.

5. Drain the vegetables and serve as finger food. Fork-mash if desired.

**2 Servings**

2 red potatoes
4 cups water
1 tablespoon mayonnaise
1 tablespoon yogurt
½ teaspoon sugar
½ teaspoon prepared
    mustard
dash of salt
dash of garlic powder

# Potato Salad

*Potato salad "dressing" can be made in any number of ways. For young eaters, go for simple ingredients, and fewer of them. Also, stay away from heavily seasoned, spiced, or salty variations, and avoid adding little bits of hard celery or pickles that toddlers could choke on. Stick to soft, easily recognizable ingredients.*

* * * * *

1.  Wash and peel the potatoes. Cut out any bad spots; then dice into small pieces.

2.  Place the potatoes in a medium saucepan and cover with water. Bring to a boil and cook for 25–30 minutes, or until potatoes are soft.

3.  Drain the potatoes and allow to cool.

4.  In a small bowl, mix the mayonnaise, yogurt, sugar, mustard, garlic powder, and salt. Gently toss with the potatoes.

5.  Chill before serving. Fork-mash if desired.

### Hot or Cold?
*Some potato salads are meant to be served hot, such as German potato salad. It's usually prepared with an oil-and-vinegar dressing, rather than the creamy dressing typical of cold potato salad. This variation may be a little too sour for your toddler, but it's certainly worth trying! Just be sure to serve it warm, not hot, to avoid burning your toddler's tongue.*

# Cheesy Twice-Baked Potatoes

*Twice-baked potatoes are a popular dish for the entire family, and a great way to use up leftover baked potatoes. When cooking for the rest of the family, you might incorporate bacon crumbles and diced green onion to the potato before rebaking, and also add a dash of salt and pepper.*

●　●　●　●　●

1. Scrub the potato thoroughly with a vegetable brush. Cut out any bad spots.

2. Pat the potato dry with a paper towel; then poke 8–10 holes into the potato, using a fork or other sharp implement. Bake at 400°F for 1 hour.

3. Once the potato has cooled, slice it open and carefully remove the potato flesh.

4. Mix the potato with the Cheddar, cream cheese, and butter. Stir well, then put it back inside the potato shell. Bake at 350°F for another 15–20 minutes.

5. Slice into strips before serving, or remove the potato skin entirely. Fork-mash if desired.

## 2 Servings

1 russet potato
1 tablespoon cream cheese
1 ounce shredded Cheddar
½ tablespoon butter

1 medium red potato
1 teaspoon oil
⅛ teaspoon salt
⅛ teaspoon basil
½ teaspoon
    Parmesan,optional

# Baked Healthy Fries

*While it's temping to share your fast-food French fries with your toddler, it's not the best idea on a regular basis. The salt and fat levels of commercially prepared fries are most unhealthful, and some fries are sized just right to be a choking hazard.*

•  •  •  •  •

1.  Preheat the oven to 400°F.

2.  Wash and scrub the potato with a vegetable brush. Cut out any bad spots, then slice into strips.

3.  Place the potatoes in a zippered plastic baggie. Add the oil, salt, basil, and cheese, and toss thoroughly to coat.

4.  Spread the potatoes on a greased baking sheet. Bake for 15 minutes, then turn each fry over and bake for another 15 minutes. Fries should be cooked but not burned or overly crispy, as toddlers without a full set of teeth won't be able to chew them.

5.  Allow fries to cool; then serve as finger-food. Supervise closely to prevent choking.

### Finishing Touches

*Many restaurants pour on the salt after their fries are finished cooking. The logic here is that the salt will adhere easily to a freshly oiled, cooked potato. True, but toddlers don't need extra salt. Try seasoning the fries for toddlers before cooking; if the rest of the family complains that they're too bland, you can always add a dash of salt and paprika later.*

# Carrot-Yam Bake

*Fresh warm pie has a special place in most people's hearts around the holidays, but there's no reason why toddlers can't enjoy this recipe year-round. It's essentially a sweet-potato pie minus the pie crust, which makes it a perfect dish for young eaters. If serving to grownups, add ½ cup sugar and pour the mixture into a pie shell before baking.*

* * * * *

**2 Servings**

1 carrot
1 small yam or sweet potato
4 cups water
1 egg
1 tablespoon butter or
   margarine, melted
2 tablespoons milk (regular
   or soy)

1. Wash and peel the yam and carrot. Dice into chunks.

2. Place in a pot of water and bring to a boil. Cook for 30–35 minutes, or until soft.

3. Preheat oven to 350°F. Drain the vegetables and mash with a fork.

4. Beat the egg and milk together; then mix with the vegetables. Stir in the butter.

5. Bake in a greased ovenproof dish for 45 minutes, or until the vegetables are set and fully cooked. Allow to cool before serving.

2 cups fresh leafy greens or
    ½ cup cooked spinach
½ apple
3 cups water

# Spinach with Apples

*Depending on how readily available fresh spinach is in your area, frozen spinach may or may not be a time-saver. In the bagged-salad section of most grocery stores, you can find spinach year-round, and it actually takes less time to cook than it does to thaw frozen spinach. Also, if you only need a small amount, using fresh spinach ensures little waste.*

●   ●   ●   ●   ●

1. Wash the spinach leaves thoroughly, removing any damaged parts.

2. Wash and peel the apple, removing the core and seeds. Dice into small chunks.

3. Place the apple in a medium saucepan and cover with water. Bring to a boil and cook for 15–20 minutes, or until apples are starting to soften.

4. Add the spinach and more water, if necessary. Return to a boil; then cook for 10–15 minutes, or until spinach is thoroughly cooked.

5. Fork-mash if desired.

### The Salad Version

*When making a grown-up dish using the same recipe, how about a spinach and apple salad? Chop fresh spinach leaves and apples, and throw in ½ cup raisins and walnuts. Serve with a light dressing of olive oil, balsamic vinegar, and a dash of salt, sugar, pepper, and dry mustard.*

# Peaches and Sweet Potatoes

*While straight cinnamon smells fantastic, it usually has a slightly bitter taste. To get the flavor of the cinnamon without the bitter overtone, recipes almost always instruct mixing it with sugar. By the same token, although nutmeg smells fantastic, a little goes a long way, and without a touch of something sweet, too much nutmeg will make for a bitter meal.*

• • • • •

**2 Servings**

1 small peach
1 small yam or sweet potato, diced
4 cups water
⅛ teaspoon nutmeg
⅛ teaspoon cinnamon
⅛ teaspoon sugar

1. Place the sweet potato in a pot of water and bring to a boil. Cook for about 15 minutes.

2. Wash and peel the peach. Cut into thin slices and add to the pot with the sweet potato. Cook for another 15–20 minutes. Sprinkle the cinnamon, sugar, and nutmeg into the cooking water.

3. When cooked, drain the peach and sweet potato and allow to cool. Serve as finger food or fork-mash if desired.

# Smashed Potatoes

*Smashed potatoes are typically lumpier than mashed potatoes and are often browned in a pan before serving. A 2-year-old may have fun with the one-sided crispiness of the smashed potatoes.*

• • • • •

**1 Serving**

1 red potato, diced
1 tablespoon oil
3 cups water
dash of salt and pepper, optional

1. Place the potato in a saucepan, cover with water, and bring to a boil. Cook for 30–35 minutes, or until soft.

2. Drain the potatoes. Heat the oil in the saucepan and add the potatoes again. When they start to brown, smash with a fork or potato masher. If desired, add a dash of salt and pepper while smashing.

3. Allow to cool before serving.

## 2 Servings

*1 plum or small beefsteak tomato*
*1 ounce Mozzarella, shredded*

# Cheesy Tomatoes

*Try serving this dish with rice or pasta. Or, prepare a plate of white rice or noodles; then microwave the tomatoes with cheese right on top for a one-dish meal.*

●　●　●　●　●

1.  Wash the tomato and cut into rings about ⅛ inch thick each. Top with shredded cheese.

2.  Place the tomato-cheese slices on a microwaveable plate. Cook for 10 seconds or until the cheese is melted. Serve either whole or cut into quarters.

### Oven Instead

*If you're already using the oven for another dish for the family, Cheesy Tomatoes can be made just as easily by baking. Simply put them on a greased baking sheet and cook until the cheese melts. Cook them at 400°F for 5 minutes, or adjust the time accordingly for whatever temperature your oven is set to.*

# Peas with Mint

*Mint is both refreshing and medicinal. If your toddler is having an upset stomach or seems irritable from gas, adding a bit of mint to his diet may be just the thing. Mint may have a curative effect on nausea, headache, and other various ailments. Plus, it smells great while cooking and tastes even better.*

•  •  •  •  •

1. Chop the fresh mint into tiny pieces.

2. Place the peas in a pot of water and bring to a boil. Cook for 8–10 minutes, or until the peas are soft.

3. Drain the water and return the peas to the pot. Add the butter, stirring constantly until the butter melts.

4. Add the chopped mint and mix. Serve as is or fork-mash if desired.

**1 Serving**

*½ cup peas*
*2 cups water*
*3 leaves fresh mint*
*½ tablespoon butter*

# Yogurt Fruit Drink

*Here is a healthy summer drink. It could even be made into a winter drink! Simply substitute whatever fruit is in season—it's hard to go wrong with puréed fruit and yogurt. If you're out of fruit, use fruit juice instead.*

•  •  •  •  •

1. Hull and clean the strawberries. Cut in half.

2. Wash and peel the peach. Remove the pit; cut into pieces.

3. Peel the banana and remove any damaged spots. Cut into chunks.

4. Place strawberries, peach, banana, and yogurt in the blender. Mix until a thin drink results.

5. Add water as needed, 1 tablespoon at a time, if too thick.

**2 Servings**

*1 cup vanilla yogurt*
*2 strawberries*
*1 peach*
*½ banana*

2 asparagus spears
2 cups of water
½ ripe avocado
1 tablespoon cottage cheese

# Asparagus Cheese Dip

*Asparagus dip is a great way to use up leftover asparagus. This dip is high in vitamin C, vitamin K, and folate, which makes this recipe terrific for pregnant women too. The folate is also beneficial for your toddler's cardiovascular system, and asparagus is generally considered one of nature's most beneficial vegetables.*

●　●　●　●　●

1. Bring the asparagus and water to a boil in a shallow saucepan. Steam for 10–15 minutes, or until the asparagus is soft.

2. Cut the avocado in half. Remove the pit and scoop the avocado out of the skin. Cut into chunks and place into a food processor or blender.

3. When the asparagus is cooked, chop into pieces and add to the food processor.

4. Add the cottage cheese to the food processor and purée until the mixture is smooth. If it's too thick, add cooking water from the asparagus, 1 tablespoon at a time.

5. Serve as a dipping sauce. Refrigerate the leftovers immediately.

### Dippers
*Toddlers may want to dip their fingers (or entire hands) into this recipe—and that's okay! But if you're looking for a cleaner dipper than a human body part, try the Whole-Wheat Teething Crackers on page 91. Bread crusts make excellent tools for dipping. Also, try well-cooked baby carrots as dippers; they're firm enough for toddlers to handle, and soft enough to chew.*

# Tomato Risotto

*The best thing about risotto is that it's soft — perfect for toddlers without a full mouthful of teeth. The sauce is cooked right into the rice, yielding an easy-to-make dish that's very flavorful. While usually made with arborio rice, risotto can also be made with carnaroli or vialone nano. These are particularly starchy grains that give risotto its creamy texture.*

●　●　●　●　●

**1 Serving**

½ cup arborio rice
1 tablespoon butter or
    margarine
½ cup tomato
⅔ cup chicken stock or water
¼ cup grated Parmesan,
    optional

1. Wash the tomato and dice into small pieces. Alternatively, use canned diced tomatoes, and manually dice into smaller pieces. Reserve all juices.

2. Bring the chicken stock and tomatoes to a boil. Add the rice and reduce heat to simmering.

3. Cover and cook for 20–25 minutes, or until all liquid is absorbed. When preparing this dish for older children or adults, cook the risotto about 5 minutes less so the rice is firmer.

4. Stir in the Parmesan and the butter once the rice is fully cooked. Either serve as is or fork-mash if desired.

**1 Serving**

*1 medium red potato*
*3 cups water*
*½ cup fresh spinach leaves*
*1 cabbage leaf*
*1 ounce Cheddar, shredded*

# Cheese Colcannon

*Colcannon is a British and Irish dish that usually involves potatoes and cabbage. While this dish can be made in bulk using the slow cooker, it's just as easy (and a lot faster) to boil on the stove when making a small amount. To make the dish more authentic, add a bit of parsnip and leeks, but these vegetables may be a bit stronger tasting.*

•   •   •   •   •

1.  Wash and peel the potato. Dice.

2.  Place the potato in a medium saucepan and cover with water. Bring to a boil; then cook for about 20 minutes.

3.  Add the cabbage and spinach to the saucepan. Return to a boil, and continue cooking for another 10 minutes.

4.  Drain the vegetables; then fork-mash until they are combined.

5.  Add in the shredded cheese and continue fork-mashing until the cheese is incorporated.

### Hold the Mace

*Traditional colcannon is seasoned with mace, an Indonesian spice that is similar to nutmeg (and actually comes from the same tree as nutmeg). Mace may be difficult to find, can be expensive, and its flavor isn't always one that young children find appealing. If you're inclined, try adding ⅛ teaspoon while fork-mashing the vegetables together.*

# Chickpea and Tomato Salad

*Garbanzo beans, also called chickpeas, are a great staple for toddlers because they're mild in flavor and high in protein. This is also an easy summer dish because it can be served raw—no cooking required! Cooking the chickpeas won't make them much softer, so be sure to fork-mash thoroughly. Cooking the tomatoes will soften them, so feel free to cook them for 10–15 minutes before using.*

●  ●  ●  ●  ●

1. Drain the garbanzo beans and rinse well.

2. Wash the tomato and remove the stem and any tough white flesh. Dice into small pieces.

3. In a small bowl, mix together the oil, vinegar, sugar, and lemon juice.

4. Toss the dressing with the garbanzo beans, tomatoes, and parsley. Fork-mash before serving. If your toddler seems averse to the sourness of the vinegar, either omit it or skip the dressing entirely.

**2 Servings**

½ cup canned garbanzo beans
½ cup tomato
1 tablespoon parsley
1 teaspoon olive oil
1 teaspoon red wine vinegar
½ teaspoon sugar
¼ teaspoon lemon juice

## Carrot Pancakes

**4 Servings**

1 carrot
1 cup all-purpose flour
½ cup milk or water
1 egg
4 teaspoons oil
1 teaspoon baking powder

*While most toddlers naturally like vegetables, some may take a little extra encouragement. Try this recipe, which makes carrots into fun pancakes! While grown-up tastes might prevent dousing these pancakes with maple syrup, it could be a tempting taste for a toddler, so give it a try. Serve as a breakfast, lunch, or dinner food.*

• • • • •

1. Wash and peel the carrot, and remove both ends. Grate the remainder.

2. Mix the flour, egg, baking powder, milk, and 1 teaspoon oil in a medium bowl. When it forms a batter, stir in the grated carrot.

3. Heat 1 tablespoon of oil in a frying pan. Drop spoonfuls of batter into the heated oil. The resulting pancakes should be 1–2 inches in diameter. Cook 2–3 minutes, or until browned. Flip and cook 2–3 minutes on the other side.

4. Drain onto paper towels. Serve as finger food once cooled.

**Up the Protein**
*Looking for a good way to increase the protein in your child's diet? Try adding cooked chickpeas to the grated carrots before frying. Simply purée ½ cup chickpeas in the food processor; then mix by hand with the carrots and form small patties. They taste delicious and provide a healthful meat alternative.*

# Baby's Vegetable Casserole

### 3 Servings

½ cup broccoli
½ cup zucchini
½ cup cauliflower
1 small carrot
4 cups water
1 tablespoon butter
½ cup shredded Cheddar

*Vegetable casseroles can be prepared in any number of ways. Many have crunchy toppings, which are great for older kids but less appropriate for toddlers. If you like, crush up some butter-flavored crackers and place on top of half the dish. Dot with butter, and bake for the same amount of time. Half the dish will be fine for a toddler, and half will be suited for an older audience.*

●　●　●　●　●

1. Wash the broccoli and cauliflower. Dice into small florets.

2. Wash and peel the carrot and zucchini; then dice into small coins.

3. Put carrot in a medium saucepan. Add 3 cups of water, bring to a boil, and cook for 10 minutes. Add the broccoli, cauliflower, and zucchini and cook another 10–15 minutes, or until the vegetables are soft.

4. Drain the vegetables; then add the butter and cheese. Stir until melted, tossing the vegetables to ensure an even coating.

5. Pour into a greased dish about the size of a loaf pan. Bake at 350°F for 30 minutes. Allow to cool; then either serve as is or fork-mash if desired.

**3 Servings**

¾ cup broccoli
2 cups water
½ cup Mozzarella
1 egg
¼ cup bread crumbs
2 tablespoons oil

# Broccoli and Cheese Nuggets

*A healthy meat-free alternative to fast-food chicken nuggets, these balls can be oven-baked instead of fried. Frying may be neater in the end, however. Cheese melts quickly in the oven, so frying, with its faster cooking time, better preserves the shape of the nuggets.*

•　•　•　•　•

1. Wash the broccoli and dice into small pieces. Cover with water in a saucepan and bring to a boil. Cook for 15 minutes, or until the broccoli is tender. Drain and let cool; then either purée in a food processor or fork-mash.

2. Grate the Mozzarella, and mix it with the cooked mashed broccoli. Pour in a beaten egg and mix thoroughly to combine.

3. Tightly mold a small ball of broccoli and cheese with your hands. Roll it in bread crumbs to cover on all sides, and place on a plate. Repeat until all the balls are made.

4. Heat the oil in a frying pan. When hot, carefully place the broccoli-cheese balls into the pan. Fry for 1–2 minutes; turn over with a spatula. Let fry for another 1–2 minutes; turn over again. Nuggets are cooked when all sides are lightly browned.

5. Drain onto paper towels. Serve as finger food once cooled.

### It's All in the Oil
*There are several types of oil you can use for cooking. Canola oil is relatively high in monounsaturated fat and low in saturated fat, so it is an excellent choice for cooking. Vegetable oil (which is generally made from soybean oil) has less "good fat." Sunflower oil has a high amount of protein, and is particularly good for frying.*

# Cheesy Corn Nuggets

*Sometimes known as fritters, corn nuggets are usually deep fried, but can be made healthier by pan frying in a small amount of oil. These fried delights, when made with buttermilk and cornmeal, are also called hush puppies in some southern parts of the United States.*

• • • • •

**4 Servings**

1 cup corn (canned or 3 ears
    fresh corn), cooked
¼ cup shredded Cheddar
1 egg
2 tablespoons flour
½ tablespoon butter, melted
2 tablespoons oil

1. Shave the corn off the sides of ears of cooked corn, yielding 1 cup of corn kernels. Mash it well with a fork or run it through the food processor.

2. Whisk the egg in a medium bowl. Add the flour, melted butter, shredded cheese, and corn, mixing thoroughly to combine.

3. Heat the oil in a frying pan. When hot, drop the batter into the pan by the spoonful, leaving enough space between them so that the fritters do not touch.

4. Let fry 2–3 minutes; then flip over with a spatula. Cook another 2–3 minutes, flipping again if necessary.

5. Drain onto paper towels. Serve as finger food once cooled.

**1 Serving**

¼ cup sugar-snap peas
¼ cup pearl onions
1 tablespoon butter
½ cup water

# Sautéed Sugar-Snap Peas with Onions

*Of the many types of onions, pearl onions are one of the best suited for serving to toddlers. Other mild-flavored onions include the yellow Bermuda onion, the white Spanish onion, and the red Italian onion. Any of these can be substituted for pearl onions in this recipe, though you may want to cut the amount in half so that the onion flavor does not overpower the peas.*

●　●　●　●　●

1. Cut each pearl onion into quarters.

2. Melt the butter in a deep frying pan; then add the onions. Cook over medium heat for several minutes, stirring constantly to prevent burning or sticking.

3. If using fresh pea pods, select ones that are firm, bright green, and medium size. Snap off the ends, and remove the strings from each pea. Or substitute frozen sugar-snap peas.

4. Add the water and peas into the frying pan. Bring to a boil; then simmer for 10–15 minutes, or until peas are cooked and tender.

5. Allow to cool; then either serve as is or fork-mash if desired.

## Pearl Onions

*As the name suggests, pearl onions are very small, round white onions. They're typically ½–1 inch in diameter and are the primary onion used in making pickled onions. They're good for introducing onions to toddlers because they're relatively mild and sweet.*

# Tuna with Vegetables

*Canned tuna is typically available in several varieties: flaked, grated, chunk, and solid packed. It is also sold with different packing liquids, including water, vegetable oil, or broth. Oil-packed tuna will naturally be greasier than the tuna packed in water and is much higher in fat; when cooking for babies, use tuna packed in water.*

* * * * *

1. Drain tuna and mash into small pieces.

2. Wash and peel the carrot, then dice into small pieces. Place in a saucepan, cover with water, and bring to a boil. Cook for about 10 minutes.

3. Add the peas to the pot and cook for another 10–12 minutes, or until vegetables are tender. Toss with a dash of garlic powder.

4. Grease a small ovenproof baking dish. Combine tuna and cooked vegetables and spread in dish. Dot with butter. Bake at 350°F for about 20 minutes, or until the fish is heated through.

5. Allow to cool; then either serve as is or fork-mash if desired.

### Fish and Mercury Warning

*White albacore tuna comes from larger fish and can be higher in mercury than chunk light tuna. It is safe to feed your baby tuna once or twice a week, and it's better to stick to chunk light tuna than albacore. Avoid shark, swordfish, king mackerel, and tilefish—these large fish commonly have high levels of mercury.*

## 2 Servings

*2 ounces canned tuna*
*½ cup peas*
*½ cup carrots*
*1 tablespoon butter*
*dash garlic powder*
*2 cups water*

*1 thin salmon fillet*
*2 tablespoons water*
*dash of dill*

# Poached Salmon

*For a meal that's quick, healthy, and easy to cook, it's hard to beat simple poached salmon. Poaching is a fast way of cooking that locks in flavor. It's also nice because it won't produce the fishy smell that's typical of frying.*

●　●　●　●　●

1.  Wash the salmon well, removing all bones.

2.  Pour the water and dill into a sautéing pan. Place the fish into the pan, putting the skin-side face-down.

3.  Bring the water to a boil. Reduce to simmering, cover the pan, and cook for 10–12 minutes, or until the fish flakes easily with a fork.

4.  Allow to cool; then do one more check for bones. Either serve as is or fork-mash if desired.

### Season the Waters

*If you'd like to try infusing a little more flavor into the fish without actually spicing it up, try seasoning the cooking water. Good additives might be a dash of salt and pepper, splash of lemon juice, and a sprig or two of parsley. Simply discard these ingredients along with the cooking water before serving your toddler.*

# Baked Fish Sticks

*Homemade fish sticks are much healthier than most frozen varieties, and they'll be easier for toddlers to chew because you're using fresh fish. The only downside, though, is that you have to make sure the fish is thoroughly deboned. If you're using a fresh whole fillet, run your fingers along with sides, feeling carefully for bones. If you feel any, slide a sharp knife underneath the bone to completely remove it.*

• • • • •

1. Preheat oven to 400°F. Grease a baking sheet or dish.

2. Rinse the fish fillet and remove all bones. Cut into slices.

3. Beat the egg and milk together in a small bowl. Place the flour in a pile on one small plate, and the bread crumbs in a pile on another small plate.

4. Dip each fish stick into flour, then egg, then Parmesan and bread crumbs. Shake gently to remove any excess and place on the baking sheet.

5. Bake for 15–18 minutes. Flip the fish sticks over halfway during cooking. Cool before serving as finger food.

### Checking Out the Locals

*If you eat locally caught fish, make sure to check any warnings about mercury that might be available for fish in your area. If no warnings are available, stick to 1–2 meals of local fish per week.*

**1 Serving**

1 whitefish fillet
1 egg
½ cup milk
¼ cup bread crumbs
¼ cup all-purpose flour
1 tablespoon Parmesan

## 2 Servings

*4 ounces turkey, ground*
*1 tablespoon onion, diced*
*⅛ teaspoon prepared*
*     mustard*
*½ tablespoon oil*

# Ground Turkey

*Why offer your toddler ground turkey instead of ground beef? Two simple reasons: health and variety. Turkey is generally lower in fat than ground beef, so it's a good choice for the entire family. In addition, most recipes for spaghetti sauce, lasagna and other meat dishes use ground beef—so why not introduce a new flavor?*

* * * * *

1.  Heat the oil in a frying pan. Add onion and sauté for 4–5 minutes, or until the onion is translucent.

2.  Mix the turkey and mustard in a small bowl. Add to the frying pan and sauté for 8-10 minutes, or until the meat is completely cooked.

3.  Allow to cool; then either serve as is or fork-mash if desired.

### Turkey Combinations
*Because of its low fat content, ground turkey can be drier than fattier meats like ground beef. For this reason, especially with small children, it's a good idea to add it into a sauce. If preparing "stand-alone" ground turkey into patties, add liquid ingredients such as Worcestershire sauce, prepared mustard, or milk—they will make the meat more tender.*

# Chicken with Apricots

**2 Servings**

1 small boneless, skinless
      chicken breast (about
      6 ounces)
1 apricot
1 tablespoon apricot
      preserves
½ tablespoon butter

*One way to save time with this recipe is to use canned apricots instead of fresh. Since canned apricots already have a fair amount of juice, you can also omit the preserves. Simply take 3–4 apricot halves and about a tablespoon of juice, dice into small pieces, and pour on top of the chicken before baking.*

•  •  •  •  •

1. Wash the chicken breast and remove any skin or fat. Place in the bottom of a greased baking dish.

2. Dice the apricot into small pieces. Mix with the apricot preserves; then spread over the chicken.

3. Dot the top of the chicken with butter; then bake at 350°F for 30 minutes, or until the chicken's internal temperatures reaches 170°F. The juice from the chicken should run clear when pricked with a fork, and the chicken meat should not be pink when sliced.

4. Allow to cool; then dice into small pieces for your baby to self-feed. You can also fork-mash if desired.

1 small boneless skinless
   chicken breast (about
   6 ounces)
1 thin slice of cheese (less
   than 1 ounce)
1 tablespoon all-purpose
   flour
1 tablespoon oil
¼ cup applesauce
   (homemade or jarred)

# Chicken with Applesauce

*While jarred applesauce is perfectly acceptable for this recipe, making your own isn't much trouble either. Try serving this chicken with the Applesauce recipe on page 15. The chicken will also go well with the Peach Sauce recipe on page 16 or the Pear Sauce on page 18. Just about any sweet fruit sauce will go nicely with stuffed chicken.*

•　•　•　•　•

1.  Wash the chicken breast and remove any skin or fat. Cut a long diagonal slit across the widest part of the breast and push the cheese inside.

2.  Dip the chicken breast into flour, coating all sides. Shake gently to remove any excess.

3.  Heat the oil in a skillet. Slide the chicken breast into the hot oil and cook for 3–4 minutes, or until the first side is browned. Flip the breast and cook another 3–4 minutes. Continue cooking until the breast is completely cooked.

4.  Heat the oven to 350°F. Place the cooked chicken onto a greased cookie sheet. Pour applesauce on top and bake for 15–20 minutes, or until the applesauce is heated through.

5.  Allow to cool, cut into small pieces, and serve. You can also fork-mash if desired.

### The Art of Stuffing

*Stuffing chicken breasts is one of cooking's more laborious arts, but it's a worthy endeavor when you're experimenting with new recipes to tickle your child's taste buds. The trick to stuffing is aiming low; don't make a huge incision that might run all the way through the meat, and don't try to cram it too full or the stuffing will come out during cooking.*

# Chicken with Bananas

*We often think of bananas as breakfast and snack foods, but why not for lunch or dinner too? Many Caribbean cultures cook with bananas on a regular basis. Try this simple chicken and banana recipe, which is sure to appeal to a banana-loving toddler.*

* * * * *

1. Preheat the oven to 350°F. Wash the chicken breast and remove any skin or fat.

2. Brush both sides of the breast with butter. Place in a greased dish.

3. Peel the banana and remove any damaged spots. Cut into thin slices and place on top of the chicken. Drizzle the remaining melted butter on top of the bananas.

4. Bake for 30 minutes, or until the chicken's internal temperature reaches 170°F and the juice from the chicken runs clear when pricked with a fork.

5. Allow to cool, cut into small pieces, and serve. You can also fork-mash if desired.

**2 Servings**

1 small boneless, skinless chicken breast (about 6 ounces)
1 banana
2 tablespoons butter, melted

3 ounces ham, cooked
½ ripe peach
1 tablespoon butter
1 teaspoon honey

# Ham and Peaches

*Make sure that honey is only served to children older than 12
months old because there's a risk of botulism for younger babies.
Honey is okay for toddlers and older children.*

● ● ● ● ●

1. Wash the peach and cut in half. Peel the half you're using for this recipe, remove the pit, and dice into small pieces. Either cut a wedge out of a ham steak, use leftovers from a baked ham, or use 2 thin slices of deli-style ham.

2. Melt the butter in a medium skillet. Add the ham and sauté for several minutes, or until both sides are lightly browned. Add the honey and continue cooking another 1–2 minutes.

3. Add the diced peach to the skillet. Cook for 4–5 minutes, stirring constantly to prevent sticking or burning. Allow to cool; then either serve as is or fork-mash if desired.

# Ham and Applesauce

**1 Serving**

*3 ounces of ham, cooked*
*¼ cup applesauce*
*(homemade or jarred)*

*Ham is tender and is an easy first meat for babies to practice swallowing. Because of the curing process it's saltier than other meats, so serve in moderation.*

*●   ●   ●   ●   ●*

1. Either cut a wedge out of a ham steak, use leftovers from a baked ham, or take 2 thin slices of deli-style ham.

2. Place ham in a greased baking dish. Cover with applesauce.

3. Bake at 325°F for about 30 minutes. Allow to cool; then either serve as is or fork-mash if desired.

### Glazes

*It's fine to serve your toddler leftover glazed ham, as long as you avoid serving him the tough outer rinds. He can try maple-glazed ham, honey-glazed ham, or brown sugar–glazed ham. Your toddler will probably enjoy the sweet taste. If the glaze has raisins, supervise carefully to prevent choking.*

## 2 Servings

1 small boneless, skinless
    chicken breast (about
    6 ounces)
2 thin slices of ham
2 ounces cheese, shredded
2 tablespoons bread crumbs
1 tablespoon butter, melted

# Baby's Cordon Bleu

*When making a stuffed chicken or stuffed beef dish, a meat mallet is important because it will both flatten and tenderize the meat. A meat mallet is basically a perforated wooden or metal block, usually attached to a wooden handle. Simply place the meat on an appropriate work surface, and pound it with the mallet.*

* * * * *

1. Preheat the oven to 350°F. Wash the chicken breast and remove any skin or fat.

2. Slice the chicken breast in half horizontally. Pound with a meat mallet to make the chicken as thin as possible.

3. Place the ham slices over one piece of chicken. Sprinkle the cheese on top; then place the other piece of chicken on top.

4. Place the assembly in a greased baking dish. Brush with melted butter and sprinkle the top with bread crumbs. Bake for 40 minutes, or until the chicken's internal temperature reaches 170°F. The juice from the chicken should run clear when pricked with a fork.

5. Allow to cool, cut into small pieces, and serve. You can also fork-mash if desired.

# Chicken with Spinach

*Stir-frying is a healthy way to cook for children, especially when using minimal oil and a nonstick skillet. If you stir-fry with no cooking liquid, the meat and vegetables may ended up crisper than your baby would like. Adding a little stock or water alleviates that problem.*

* * * * *

**2 Servings**

1 small boneless, skinless chicken breast (about 6 ounces)
1 tablespoon oil
1 cup fresh spinach (or ¼ cup pre-cooked)
¼ teaspoon parsley
½ cup chicken stock or water
⅛ teaspoon pepper

1. Wash the chicken breast and remove any fat. Dice into small pieces.

2. Heat the oil in a non-stick skillet or wok. Add the chicken and stir-fry for 8–10 minutes or until chicken is no longer pink in the middle.

3. Add the spinach, chicken stock, parsley, and pepper. Continue to stir-fry an additional 4–5 minutes.

4. Allow to cool; either serve as is or fork-mash if desired.

**Add the Flavor In!**
*A quick way to add a little flavor to stir-fried chicken is to add a little sesame oil with the cooking oil. This will give the meal a great roasted-sesame flavor, without having to add sesame seeds (which are small enough not to be a choking hazard, but require careful attention for roasting).*

## 1 Serving

*¼ cup frozen orange juice concentrate*

*¼ cup frozen lemonade concentrate*

*½ banana*

*¼ cup raspberries or strawberries*

*½ cup water*

# Fruit Slush

*Frozen juice concentrates are a flexible, if not highly creative, ingredient for frozen fruit drinks. The leftovers can easily be refrozen or made into juice at a later date. It's fine to substitute any of the juices, as long as your toddler has tried all the ingredients separately and has shown no sign of allergy.*

•  •  •  •  •

1. Mix the fruit juice concentrates and water into a freezer-safe bowl or cup.

2. Peel the banana and remove any damaged spots. Fork-mash and mix into the cup of juice and water.

3. Freeze for at least 1 hour.

4. When ready to serve, thaw to the "slush stage" and stir.

### Alternates

*A more traditional method of making fruit slushes is to put ice cubes and various fruits into a blender. Frozen juice concentrate, on the other hand, is faster to prepare but generally requires more waiting time while the concentrates either freeze or thaw to the right consistency.*

# Banana Smoothie

**1 Serving**

½ ripe banana
½ cup vanilla yogurt
(regular or soy)
½ cup orange juice

*Tired of cleaning out the food processor? This recipe can be made almost as easily in a regular cup. Simply fork-mash the banana until it's creamy, and then mix in the yogurt and water with a spoon.*

* * * * *

1. Peel the banana and remove any damaged spots. Cut into slices and place in a blender or food processor.

2. Add the juice and yogurt.

3. Blend until the drink is completely smooth.

4. Refrigerate any leftover drink immediately.

## For the Older Crowd
*If you're whipping up this drink for grownups, there are a couple of small additions you could make to improve on the flavor and texture. Try using crushed ice instead of orange juice, and add a touch of banana liqueur. You can also add a bit of lemon juice, or serve it with a slice of lemon in the glass—the acidity will make a pleasing contrast to the banana.*

**2 Servings**

½ ripe banana
¼ cup yogurt (regular or soy)
¼ cup milk (regular or soy)
½ cup carrot juice

# Carrot-Banana Smoothie

*Here's an excellent way for your child to drink her fruits and vegetables! Many toddlers like carrot juice, so there's no reason not to incorporate it into a fun, summery drink.*

●　　●　　●　　●　　●

1. Peel the banana and remove any damaged spots. Cut into slices and place in a blender or food processor.

2. Stir the yogurt well; then add it into the food processor. Then add the milk and carrot juice. Note that soy milk and soy yogurt are perfectly acceptable substitutes for dairy products in this recipe.

3. Blend until the drink is completely smooth.

4. Refrigerate any leftover drink immediately.

# Berry Smoothie

*Feel good about serving your child a super-healthy beverage. The yogurt has aci-dophilus and other live cultures to aid a happy tummy, and berries (particularly blueberries) are known for their potential cancer-fighting abilities.*

**2 Servings**

½ ripe banana
½ cup yogurt (regular or soy)
¼ cup apple juice
2 large strawberries
¼ cup raspberries or blueberries

⚫ ⚫ ⚫ ⚫ ⚫

1.  Peel the banana and remove any damaged spots. Cut into slices and place in a blender or food processor.

2.  Wash the berries and remove all stems. Cut in half and place in the food processor. You can use either frozen or fresh berries.

3.  Add the juice and yogurt.

4.  Blend until the drink is completely smooth.

5.  Refrigerate any leftover drink immediately.

### Why Banana?

*Bananas are in most smoothie recipes because they help with the texture—they make a smoothie thicker and creamier than it would be with only yogurt. Without banana, a smoothie would be more of a slushie, or an iced fruit drink.*

⅓ cup honeydew
⅓ cup cantaloupe
⅓ cup watermelon
½ cup apple juice

# Melon Smoothie

*If melon isn't in season, don't despair. Frozen melon is just fine for making a
frozen fruit drink. You can also make your own frozen fruit! Next time you buy
a watermelon, cut up a few cups worth into chunks and pop it into the freezer.
That way, you'll have fruit ready to use whenever you need it.*

●　●　●　●　●

1.  Cut the honeydew in half and remove all seeds. Cut out about ⅓ cup of
    melon chunks. Place in a food processor or blender.

2.  Cut the cantaloupe in half and remove all seeds. Cut out about ⅓ cup
    of melon chunks. Add to the food processor.

3.  Take a wedge of watermelon and remove all seeds, both white and
    black. Cut out ⅓ cup of chunks and add to the food processor.

4.  Add the apple juice and blend until the drink is completely smooth. If
    the drink is too thick, add more juice by the tablespoon. If it's too thin,
    add more fruit or a tablespoon of yogurt.

5.  Refrigerate any leftover drink immediately.

# Basic Chocolate Chip Cookies

*Everyone loves chocolate chip cookies. The nice thing about this recipe is that you can sneak in the healthy nutrition of whole grains by adding powdered oats.*

* * * * *

1. Preheat the oven to 350°F.

2. In a medium bowl, cream the shortening, and sugar together. Mix with a fork until large crumbles are formed, or use an electric mixer.

3. Add the egg and mix well. Add in the flour, salt, and baking soda, continuing to stir until a dough is formed.

4. Add oatmeal and chocolate chips. Stir well; then drop spoonfuls onto a greased baking sheet, leaving about 2 inches between each cookie. Bake for 11–14 minutes.

5. Let cool on the baking sheet for 1–2 minutes, then remove and finish cool on wire racks.

### Chewy Versus Hard

*When making cookies for toddlers, try to bake them on the soft side (rather than hard and crunchy). Don't overdo it on the baking powder or baking soda, since those ingredients tend to make cookies more cake-like. Don't overcook; burning is a sure way to crisp a cookie. For really soft cookies, try using corn syrup instead of sugar.*

## 6 Servings

1 egg
½ cup shortening
⅓ cup white sugar
⅓ cup brown sugar, packed
¾ cup all-purpose flour
¼ teaspoon salt
½ teaspoon baking soda
1 cup chocolate chips
1 cup ground oats

## 5 Servings

1 egg
½ cup shortening
¼ cup white sugar
½ cup brown sugar, packed
½ teaspoon vanilla extract
½ cup all-purpose flour
¼ teaspoon salt
½ teaspoon baking soda
1½ cups rolled oats (quick or
    old-fashioned)
⅛ teaspoon cinnamon

# Basic Oatmeal Cookies

*Chewy and delicious, oatmeal cookies can have varieties that are limited only by your imagination. Once your toddler grows older, you can add dried fruit, nuts, and other tasty surprises.*

●　●　●　●　●

1.  Preheat the oven to 350°F.

2.  In a medium bowl, cream the shortening and sugars together. Mix with a fork until large crumbles are formed, or use an electric mixer.

3.  Add the egg and vanilla, mixing well. Add in the flour, cinnamon, salt, and baking soda, continuing to stir until a dough is formed.

4.  Add oatmeal. Stir well; then drop spoonfuls onto a greased baking sheet, leaving about 2 inches between each cookie. Bake for 9–11 minutes.

5.  Let cool on the baking sheet for 1–2 minutes; then remove and cool on wire racks.

½ pound ground beef
¼ cup milk or water
1 egg
2 tablespoons ketchup
1 teaspoon Worcestershire
    sauce
¼ teaspoon oregano
¼ teaspoon parsley
dash of salt and pepper
¼ cup bread crumbs
½ small onion, diced

# Meatloaf

*One of the most homey comfort foods you can imagine, meatloaf hits the spot with the entire family after a long day at school and work. This recipe is much like the "adult" version, minus the heavy seasonings.*

●　●　●　●　●

1.  Preheat the oven to 350°F.

2.  In a medium bowl, mix the ground beef, egg, and milk together. Stir well.

3.  Add in the ketchup, Worcestershire, oregano, parsley, salt, pepper, bread crumbs, and onions. Mix thoroughly to combine, using your hands if necessary.

4.  Place in an ovenproof baking dish and cook at 350°F for 1 hour. Allow to cool before slicing and serving.

### To Sauce or Not to Sauce

*A fun alternative to standard meatloaf is to coat it with a glaze. Pour ½ cup tomato sauce over the top, spread with a spoon, and bake. If tomato sauce is scarce, ketchup or honey-mustard sauce is a good substitute.*

# Mini Meatloaf

**4 Servings**

¾–1 pound ground beef
1 egg
½ cup milk or water
3 tablespoons ketchup
2 teaspoons Worcestershire
   sauce
½ teaspoon oregano
½ teaspoon parsley
dash of salt and pepper
½ cup bread crumbs
½ small onion, diced
½ cup Cheddar, shredded

*Kids love things that are just their size. These pint-sized meatloaves are perfect single-serve foods for toddlers, and the leftovers make great school lunches.*

•   •   •   •   •

1. Preheat the oven to 350°F.

2. In a medium bowl, mix the ground beef, egg, and milk together. Stir well.

3. Add in the ketchup, Worcestershire, oregano, parsley, salt, pepper, bread crumbs, and onions. Mix thoroughly to combine, using your hands if necessary.

4. Scoop equal portions into 6 muffin cups of a metal muffin tin.

5. Bake for 35–45 minutes, or until the meat is no longer pink. About 15 minutes before they're done, sprinkle Cheddar cheese on top of each mini meatloaf. Allow to cool before slicing and serving.

1 small potato, cubed
1 cup water
4 teaspoons butter or
    margarine
2 teaspoons all-purpose
    flour
½ cup milk
½ cup cooked chicken, cubed
2 tablespoons grated cheese

# Creamy Chicken and Potatoes

*This simple creamy dish combines cubes of chicken and potatoes with a creamy, cheesy sauce. Just the thing for your child to practice using his new fork on!*

●　●　●　●　●

1.  Peel the potato and cut into cubes. Place the potato in pot with water. Bring to boil, reduce heat, and simmer until tender, about 10–15 minutes. Remove from pot and drain.

2.  In a small pan, melt butter over low heat. When melted, stir in flour until well mixed. Add milk and whisk until smooth.

3.  Cook over low heat, stirring often, until sauce begins to thicken.

4.  Add potato and chicken. Stir for about 3 minutes until all ingredients are heated through.

5.  Remove pot from heat. Add cheese and stir until melted. Cool to lukewarm and serve.

# Turkey with Fruit

*Turkey fruit salad is a fun way to get kids to eat their protein and vegetables, all in one serving, and you can use up leftover turkey in the process! Adjust the seasonings as necessary to suit your child's taste.*

● ● ● ● ●

**1 Serving**

½ cup cooked turkey
2 large lettuce leaves
¼ cup grapes
¼ cup cantaloupe or honeydew melon
1 ounce Mozzarella or Cheddar, shredded
1 teaspoon olive oil
1 teaspoon white wine vinegar
dash prepared mustard

1. Tear the lettuce into small pieces and place in the bottom of a serving bowl.

2. Cut the turkey into small pieces, removing any fat and skin. Place on top of the lettuce.

3. Wash the grapes and cut in half. Cut the melon into small cubes. Mix grapes and melon in with the turkey.

4. Top with shredded cheese.

5. Prepare the dressing by mixing the oil, vinegar, and mustard. Stir well; then drizzle over the salad and mix gently.

### Grown-Up Salad Dressing

*Many children will eat vegetables with the "modified" oil-and-vinegar dressing described here. To make this dressing more suitable for adult taste buds, add a dash of garlic powder, salt, pepper, sugar, and freshly diced herbs.*

*1 egg*
*¼ cup milk or water*
*1 teaspoon Worcestershire
   sauce*
*1 pound ground beef*
*¾ cup bread crumbs*
*1 teaspoon paprika*
*dash of salt and pepper*
*½ small onion, diced*

# Meatballs

*A true family favorite, meatballs go well with boxed pasta or
Homemade Egg Pasta (page 136). They can also be served with
steamed vegetables (page 56–60) for a lower-carbohydrate meal.*

•  •  •  •  •

1. Preheat the oven to 375°F.

2. In a medium bowl, mix the egg, Worcestershire, and milk together. Beat thoroughly.

3. Add in the ground beef, bread crumbs, paprika, salt, pepper, and onions.

4. Form mixture into balls about 1 inch in diameter.

5. Place the meatballs onto a baking sheet with sides or in a deep baking dish. Bake at 375°F for 30–40 minutes, or until the meat is no longer pink.

# Stuffed Peppers

*One creative way to cook stuffed peppers is on the barbeque! Try putting them on once the heat has died down a bit, and let them cook under the cover until the pepper is soft to the touch.*

• • • • •

**2 Servings**

*1 large bell pepper
¼ pound ground beef
¼ cup tomato sauce
¼ cup cooked white or
   brown rice
1 ounce cheese, shredded
dash of salt and pepper*

1. Preheat the oven to 350°F.

2. Wash the pepper and cut off the top. Remove all seeds from the cavity.

3. Brown the ground beef in a skillet over medium heat for 10 minutes, or until it's completely cooked. Drain any fat and return beef to the pan.

4. Mix the rice, tomato sauce, cheese, salt, and pepper in with the beef. Continue cooking over low heat for 3–4 minutes, or until the cheese is melted.

5. Place the bell pepper in a deep baking dish. Pour the meat mixture inside; then bake for 1 hour, or until the green pepper is tender.

## Rice Instead

*Bell peppers can be stuffed with a variety of fillings. If your toddler doesn't like meat, try stuffing the peppers with rice, cheese, and tomatoes instead. Or, for a Southwestern twist, make a filling with corn, onions, tomatoes, and a dash of chili powder.*

## 2 Servings

½ cup cooked turkey, chopped
½ tablespoon butter
¼ cup rice
¾ cup chicken or turkey stock
¼ cup broccoli

# Chopped Turkey with Rice

*Don't happen to have any leftover turkey on hand? You can either use deli-style turkey, or purchase a turkey leg from the meat counter. Roast at 350°F for 2 hours, or until the internal temperature is 180°F.*

* * * * *

1. Wash the broccoli, cut into florets, and purée briefly in the food processor. You could also chop it into very small pieces instead.

2. Put the stock and rice into a saucepan, and bring to a boil. Add the broccoli, reduce to a simmer, and cook for 30 minutes, or per the rice package directions.

3. When the rice is cooked, add the chopped turkey and butter. Stir to mix.

4. Either serve as is or fork-mash before serving.

## 2 Servings

1 pork chop
¼ cup applesauce
1 tablespoon soy sauce
1 small clove garlic, peeled

# Stuffed Pork Chop

*An easy way to expand this recipe for a larger group of eaters is to make it with a pork roast instead of a pork chop. Simply increase the amount of applesauce in proportion to the larger size of the pork roast.*

* * * * *

1. Preheat the oven to 350°F.

2. Wash the pork chop and remove the bone. Using a sharp knife, slice the chop in half horizontally about three-fourths of the way through the chop.

3. Stuff the applesauce into the cavity.

4. Place the pork in an ovenproof baking dish. Spoon the soy sauce and garlic over the top, and bake for 40–50 minutes, or until the pork's internal temperature reaches 165°F.

5. Remove the garlic and discard. Slice pork into small pieces before serving.

# Tomato and Hamburger

*This recipe is a toddler-friendly version of a tomato-based meat sauce. Fork-mash or serve just the way it is, depending on your child's chewing abilities.*

● ● ● ● ●

1. Brown the ground beef in a skillet over medium heat for 10–15 minutes, or until completely cooked.

2. Drain any fat and return the meat to the pan.

3. Add in the tomato, green pepper, tomato sauce, chili powder, salt, and pepper. Stir well; then simmer for 10–15 minutes.

**Round It Out**

*To turn the Tomato and Hamburger recipe into a full meal, simply add pasta! Cook about ½ cup pasta in boiling water for 15–20 minutes or until cooked, and serve with the hamburger sauce. If you're a vegetarian, try making this recipe with kidney beans or black beans instead of hamburger. Skip the browning stage and go right to the simmering.*

**2 Servings**

*¼ pound ground beef
¼ cup stewed tomatoes, diced
⅛ cup tomato sauce
⅛ cup chopped green pepper
dash of chili powder
dash of salt and pepper*

*1 ounce ground turkey*
*½ cup green beans*
*1 small carrot, diced*
*¼ cup rice*
*1 tablespoon butter*
*1 cup water*

# Turkey Dinner

*Make your toddler a simple Thanksgiving dinner, any time of year!*
*This is a convenient one-skillet meal that can easily be made with leftovers.*

●　●　●　●　●

1. Wash the green beans and snap off the ends. Cut into 1-inch-long seg-ments.

2. Brown the turkey in a skillet over medium heat for 10–15 minutes, or until it's completely cooked.

3. Drain any fat and return the turkey to the skillet.

4. Add the water and butter. Bring to a boil; then add in the rice, beans, and carrots. Reduce to a simmer and cook for 30 minutes, or until rice is cooked and fluffy.

5. Check periodically to ensure that there's enough liquid. If the rice starts sticking before it's done, add ¼ cup water. Let cool before serving, and fork-mash if desired.

# Lamb with Apple

*Lamb is, compared to chicken, a relatively strong-tasting meat. However, if introduced early to toddlers and young children, it can become a favorite part of their diet.*

●　●　●　●　●

**2 Servings**

*1–2 ounces of boneless lamb*
*1 apple, diced*
*1 tablespoon butter*
*1 teaspoon turmeric*
*¼ teaspoon paprika*
*⅛ teaspoon cinnamon*

1. Cut the lamb into small pieces. Melt the butter in a skillet; then add the lamb and sauté until the meat is completely cooked, about 8–10 minutes.

2. Add the apple, turmeric, paprika, and cinnamon. Continue stir-frying for 2–3 minutes.

3. Preheat the oven to 350°F. Grease an ovenproof baking dish; then pour the lamb-and-apple mixture into a greased baking dish. Bake for 30 minutes.

4. Allow to cool before serving.

**Selection Tips**
*When selecting a good cut of beef for serving to toddlers, marbled cuts are a good choice because they are generally more tender. Not so with lamb! Because the animal is less mature, lamb is usually quite tender and doesn't require the marbled fat that beef does to make the meat tender.*

**2 Servings**

1–2 ounces of boneless lamb
½ cup pasta
1 plum tomato, diced
1 tablespoon oil
4 cups water
½ tablespoon parsley
dash of salt and pepper

# Lamb with Pasta

*Lamb is a flexible dish that tends to go well with other strong flavors, such as chili or jalapeño. Your child may not appreciate this added touch, though, so try this milder recipe that uses tomatoes in place of jalapeño.*

●  ●  ●  ●  ●

1. Bring the water to a boil in a medium saucepan. Add the pasta, and cook for 20–25 minutes or per package directions. Pasta should be very tender.

2. Cut the lamb into small pieces. Heat oil in a skillet; then add the lamb and sauté until the meat is cooked, about 8–10 minutes.

3. Wash and dice the tomato into small pieces. Add tomatoes to the lamb and stir-fry over low heat for 3–4 minutes.

4. Drain the cooked pasta. Add to the lamb skillet, along with the parsley, salt, and pepper, and stir-fry for 2–3 more minutes.

5. Allow to cool before serving.

# Sweet-and-Sour Meatballs

*Sweet-and-sour sauce doesn't need to be so powerful that it brings tears to your eyes, or makes you cringe. Especially when cooking for young children, it's important to introduce a variety of flavors—but not super-strong ones!*

* * * * *

1. Mix the ground beef, bread crumbs, and soy sauce together. Form into round 1-inch balls.

2. Heat the oil in a skillet. Add the meatballs, reduce heat to medium, and cook until the meatballs are no longer pink.

3. Put the pineapple chunks and juice (about ¼ cup) into a small bowl. Add cornstarch and water, and stir well to mix. Add in the bell pepper.

4. Pour the pineapple mixture into the skillet. Stir the meatballs around to coat in the sauce, and cook the sauce for several minutes or until it thickens.

5. Allow to cool before serving.

### Keeping It Together
*If your meatballs always fall apart when you cook on the stovetop, there are a few things you can try to help them maintain their shape. Add a little oil to the pan to keep them from sticking and falling apart when you roll them over. Also, adding more egg and bread crumbs (and pressing the meat very firmly into balls) will keep them from disintegrating into meat sauce.*

### 2 Servings

¼ pound ground beef
2 teaspoons oil
½ cup canned pineapple chunks, diced
¼ cup bell pepper, diced
½ teaspoon soy sauce
¼ cup bread crumbs
1 teaspoon cornstarch
2 tablespoons water

**2 Servings**

1 small boneless, skinless
    chicken breast (about 6
    ounces)
½ cup pasta
1 medium carrot
2 teaspoons oil
½ cup chicken stock

# Chicken, Pasta, and Carrots

*This recipe is a classic spring dish, and one that covers nearly the
entire food pyramid! Farfalle pasta is a good choice, but any
small pasta shape will cook quickly and be easy for self-feeders.*

●　●　●　●　●

1.  Wash the chicken breast and remove any skin or fat. Cut into small
    pieces.

2.  Heat the oil in a skillet. Add the chicken; then stir-fry for 10–12 minutes,
    or until the chicken is cooked.

3.  Wash and peel the carrot; slice into thin coins.

4.  Bring water to a boil. Add the carrots and cook for about 10 minutes.
    Add the pasta and cook for another 20 minutes, or until both pasta and
    carrots are tender.

5.  Drain; add the pasta and carrots into the skillet with the chicken. Add
    chicken stock and cook at a high temperature for 4–5 minutes.

### Spoon, Fork, or Spork?

*Your toddler has three main choices for feeding implements once her
fingers no longer suffice. Rubber-tipped spoons are great for feeding
purées, and dull-tined forks help more for stabbing discreet bites.
Neither seeming to work quite well enough? Try a spork, or a spoon
with tined edges. She can both scoop and stab at the same time.*

# Shepherd's Pie

*Shepherd's Pie is a traditional meal consisting of beef and vegetables, topped with mashed potatoes, and baked. Any leftover meat will work.*

● ● ● ● ●

1. Wash and peel the potatoes, then cut into chunks. Bring 4 cups of water to a boil in a medium saucepan. Add the potatoes and cook for 25–30 minutes, or until the potatoes are soft.

2. Brown the ground beef in a skillet until the meat is completely cooked, about 10–15 minutes. Drain the fat.

3. Bring 1 cup of water to a boil in a small saucepan. Add the peas and cook for 8–10 minutes, or until the peas are tender.

4. Place the drained potatoes in a bowl. Add the butter and start mashing, using either a fork or an electric mixer. Add milk, 1 tablespoon at a time, until the mashed potatoes have a creamy texture.

5. Place the ground beef and peas in a greased baking dish. Spread the mashed potatoes on top, and bake at 350°F for about 1 hour.

## 4 Servings

½ pound ground beef
½ cup peas
2 medium russet potatoes
1 tablespoon butter
½ cup milk or water
6 cups water

**3 Servings**

1 cup cooked ham, chopped
2 medium red potatoes
4 cups water
1 egg
dash of pepper
1 tablespoon oil

# Ham and Potato Patties

*Try dipping these delicious patties in mayonnaise, ketchup, melted cheese, or just eat them plain. They'll be a favorite with the kids no matter what!*

* * * * *

1.  Peel potatoes; then grate into a medium bowl. Mix grated potato with the ham and pepper.

2.  Beat the egg, pour into the ham-and-potato mixture, and stir thoroughly to combine. Form into patties.

3.  Heat the oil, and cook the patties for 3–4 minutes per side, or until lightly browned. Drain on paper towels before serving.

### Ham Hash Browns
*Another way to make ham and potato patties is to make Ham Hash Browns. Slice the cooked ham into very thin strips, then mix with grated potato and fry it in one large patty. You can even prepare the mixture the night before, store it in the refrigerator, and cook it up for a hearty morning's breakfast.*

# Baked Chicken Nuggets

*Here's a healthy solution to fried chicken nuggets. They take a little longer to bake than to pan- or deep-fry, but they're less greasy and healthier for the whole family.*

* * * * *

1. Wash the chicken breast and remove any skin or fat. Cut into bite-sized pieces.

2. If using corn flakes, crush into a fine powder. Add the parsley, garlic powder, and onion powder to bread crumbs or crushed corn flakes, and mix well.

3. Roll each piece of chicken in the crushed flakes or bread crumbs. Set on a plate.

4. Preheat the oven to 400°F. Place the breaded nuggets on a greased baking sheet and cook for about 15 minutes, or until the chicken is white when you slice into it.

5. Drain any residual grease onto paper towels, and serve once cooled.

## 2 Servings

1 small boneless, skinless chicken breast (about 6 ounces)
1 cup bread crumbs or corn flakes
½ teaspoon garlic powder
¼ teaspoon onion powder
¼ teaspoon parsley

*1 English muffin*
*2 tablespoons tomato sauce*
*1 ounce shredded*
    *Mozzarella*
*4 thin slices pepperoni*
*1 baby carrot*
*2 tablespoons peas*
*2 cups water*

# Mini Pizza Faces

*Bring a smile to your child's face with this smiling pizza meal! You can do any number of substitutions here—olives instead of pepperoni or green pepper instead of carrots. Use whatever vegetables you have on hand.*

• • • • •

1. Preheat the oven to 375°F.

2. Slice the baby carrot in half lengthwise. Place it and the peas in a saucepan with the water. Bring to a boil; then cook for about 10 minutes, or until the vegetables are tender. Drain and set aside.

3. Split the English muffin in half and lay the two pieces face-up on a baking sheet. Spoon tomato sauce over each muffin to cover it and lay a foundation for the pizza face.

4. On each muffin, place 2 pieces of pepperoni for eyes. Place half a baby carrot for a nose. Make a smile out of peas. Place the shredded Mozzarella around the top of the muffin for hair.

5. Bake for 10–15 minutes, or until the cheese melts.

### Super-Size It
*If the whole family's in the mood for pizza, simply make a full-sized pie and serve your toddler a slice. Use the same fun ingredients to make a pizza face, but use pizza dough instead of English muffins.*

# Grandma's Meat Biscuit Roll

*This innovative dish requires a little extra effort, but it's sure to please. It also makes fantastic leftovers, so feel free to double or triple the recipe.*

•   •   •   •   •

1. Preheat the oven to 350°F. Brown the ground beef in a skillet until the meat is completely cooked, about 10–15 minutes. Drain the fat.

2. Mix in the tomato sauce, parsley, and oregano. Stir well, simmer over low heat for another 5 minutes.

3. Sift the flour with the baking powder and salt (be sure there are no lumps of baking powder, or someone will be getting a rather unpleasant bite.) Work in the shortening with a fork it forms large crumbles. Add in the cold milk, 1 tablespoon at a time, and stir until a thick batter is formed. If the dough is too sticky, add more flour.

4. Roll out the dough on a floured work surface. Place the cooked meat into the middle and roll the dough up so that it folds over to make a cylinder. Place on a greased baking sheet.

5. Bake for 30 minutes, or until the biscuit is golden brown. Cut into slices before serving.

## 4 Servings

*½ pound ground beef*
*2 tablespoons tomato sauce*
*1 teaspoon parsley*
*1 teaspoon oregano*
*2 cups pastry flour*
*¼ cup shortening*
*3 teaspoons baking powder*
*¼ teaspoon salt*
*½ cup cold milk or water*

**1 Serving**

¼ cup chunk light tuna
½ cup milk (regular or soy)
1 tablespoon all-purpose
   flour
1 tablespoon butter
1 piece whole-grain bread

# Creamed Tuna on Toast

*Creamed tuna is a quick, easy meal suitable for children of all chewing abilities. If toast doesn't tickle your child's fancy, try serving with crackers or breadsticks.*

•  •  •  •  •

1. Melt the butter in a small saucepan.

2. Add the flour, stirring constantly until dissolved. Add the milk and continue stirring until it forms a thick sauce.

3. Turn off the heat and add the tuna. Stir until mixed and creamy.

4. Serve on top of a piece of whole-grain toast.

### A Sweet Touch

*Having trouble getting your toddler to eat tuna? Creamed fish recipes can be made a little sweeter by adding a touch of sugar to the white sauce. On the other hand, some prefer a dash of salt with their tuna. You can also make this meal more visually appealing by adding a handful of peas for color. Again, be careful about serving tuna too often because of the amount of mercury in it.*

# Fish Chowder

*Use any mild whitefish in this chowder recipe. Clams are typically chewy and not the best to offer a young eater, but an excellent chowder can be made with fish instead.*

* * * * *

1. Melt the butter in a medium saucepan. Once melted, add the water or fish stock.

2. Add peas, carrots, and potatoes to the saucepan.

3. Rinse the fish fillet and remove all bones. Cut into small pieces and add to the saucepan. Cook for 15–20 minutes. The fish should flake easily and the vegetables should be getting tender.

4. Add the milk, thyme, and parsley. Simmer for another 5–10 minutes. Either serve as a chunky soup, or purée in the food processor.

## 2 Servings

1 boneless fillet whitefish
1 tablespoon butter
1 small carrot, diced
1 small red potato, diced
2 tablespoons peas
⅛ teaspoon thyme, crushed
¼ teaspoon parsley
½ cup milk (regular or soy)
1 cup fish stock or water

**2 Servings**

*2 ounces sardines*
*2 teaspoons mayonnaise*
*1 teaspoon lemon juice*
*1 slice of ripe avocado*

# Sardine and Avocado Spread

*Though the strong taste of sardines might turn you off, don't assume the same for your toddler! Some children like odd, even overwhelming flavors, so give this recipe a try.*

* * * * *

1. Rinse the sardines and remove all bones.

2. Cut one good-sized slice of a ripe avocado. Fork-mash together with the sardines until both are completely mashed.

3. Add mayonnaise and lemon juice. Stir to form a creamy spread.

4. Serve on top of a piece of whole-grain bread or crackers.

### Sardine History

*Sardines were one of the first fish to be canned. Starting in the nineteenth century, sardines were canned in either oil or tomato juice. The most common type of canned sardines is herring, and they can also be purchased fresh. Because they're so small, they can be difficult to debone; if possible, use sardines that have already been deboned.*

# Tuna Fishcakes

*Fresh out of fresh tuna? Don't despair; these fishcakes can be made just as easily using a boneless fillet of whitefish such as orange roughy or sole.*

●　●　●　●　●

**2 Servings**

1 boneless fillet tuna (about
　3–4 ounces)
1 medium red potato
2 cups water or fish stock
1 egg
1 teaspoon parsley
1 tablespoon oil
½ cup bread crumbs

1. Rinse the fish fillet and remove all bones. Cut into small pieces.

2. Wash and peel the potato, then dice into small pieces.

3. Bring the water to a boil in a medium saucepan. Add the fish and potato; then cook for 20–25 minutes, or until the fish is cooked and the potato is tender.

4. Fork-mash the fish and potato in a small bowl. Add the egg and parsley, then mix thoroughly. Form into patties. Put the bread crumbs on a plate, and roll each patty in bread crumbs so that it's well-coated.

5. Heat the oil in a nonstick skillet. Sauté the patties 2–3 minutes, or until lightly browned, then flip and repeat on the other side. Drain on paper towels before serving.

## 6 Servings

1 boneless fillet whitefish
2 medium red potatoes,
    diced
1 medium carrot, diced
½ cup broccoli, diced
1 cup water
½ cup milk (regular or soy)
1 tablespoon all-purpose
    flour
1 tablespoon butter

# Fish-Potato-Broccoli Pie

*Most toddlers have difficulty with hard pie crust, so this "pie" recipe is minus the shell. Baking it in muffin tins provides single-servings and easy leftovers.*

* * * * *

1. Rinse the fish fillet and remove all bones. Cut into small pieces.

2. Bring water to a boil in a medium saucepan. Add the potatoes, carrots, and broccoli, then cook for about 10 minutes. Add the fish and cook another 10–15 minutes or until the fish flakes easily. When cooked, drain and return the fish and vegetables to the saucepan.

3. In a separate small saucepan, melt the butter. Stir in the flour. Once mixed, add in the milk and stir constantly until a thin sauce is formed. Mix this sauce in with the fish and vegetables, stirring to combine.

4. Divide the fish and vegetables into a 6-cup muffin tin. Bake at 350°F for 30 minutes. Let cool before serving, and fork-mash if desired.

### Adding a Crust

*For a more "adult" version of this recipe, try making it using a single-shell pie crust. A single pie crust is made by mixing 1⅓ cups flour with ½ cup vegetable shortening. When mixed, slowly add 3 tablespoons of ice water. Once a dough is formed, roll out and use immediately, or store in the refrigerator (wrapped in plastic) until ready for use.*

# Haddock in Orange Sauce

**2 Servings**

1 boneless fillet haddock or
    other whitefish
¼ cup orange juice
½ teaspoon orange zest

*Orange zest can be obtained from an orange peel using a zester, but don't despair if you don't have this specialized instrument. You can also rub the orange against a fine grater instead—the peel that comes off will be ground enough for use as zest.*

• • • • •

1. Preheat the oven to 350°F.

2. Rinse the fish fillet and remove all bones. Place in a greased baking dish.

3. Mix the orange juice and orange zest in a small bowl. Pour over the fish and spread the zest with a fork, making sure the fish gets an even coating.

4. Bake at 350°F for 15–20 minutes. The fish is cooked when it's opaque, and flakes easily with a fork.

5. Spoon the remaining sauce from the pan over the fish, and cut into bite-size pieces before serving.

½ small butternut squash
6 cups water or vegetable
  stock
⅛ teaspoon oregano,
  crushed
⅛ teaspoon thyme, crushed
1 small clove garlic, minced
2 medium carrots
½ small onion, diced
1 tablespoon butter or
  margarine

# Carrot and Squash Soup

*If you're looking for a creamed squash soup, that variation can easily be added to this recipe. After puréeing the soup, add ½ cup heavy cream and simmer over low heat for 5 minutes. The soup can also be made a little richer by substituting a cup of milk for the vegetable stock.*

* * * * *

1. Peel the squash, remove the seeds and pulp, and cut into chunks.

2. Melt the butter in a large saucepan. Add the onion and garlic, sautéing until the onion becomes translucent.

3. Add the squash, carrot, and vegetable stock. Bring to a boil; then add oregano and thyme. Reduce to a simmer and cook for 1–2 hours, or until the vegetables are tender.

4. When the soup is done, purée in a food processor or blender before serving.

### Why Purée a Soup?

*Some soups are meant to be eaten. Minestrone soup, for example, has bites of beans, pasta, and other items that have their own distinct textures. Tomato and squash soup, though, are examples of soups that are best served with a smooth texture. These soups are well accompanied by toast, crackers, or breadsticks for dipping.*

# Vegetable Soup

*Vegetable soup is one of the most flexible recipes out there. Use chicken, vegetable, or beef stock for added flavor—black beans or chickpeas instead of kidney beans are acceptable substitutes as well. Clean out your vegetable drawer while creating several healthy meals for your toddler!*

*     *     *     *     *

1. Snap the ends off the green beans, and then cut into 1-inch segments.

2. Melt the butter in a large saucepan. Add the onion, and sauté until it becomes translucent.

3. Add potato, carrot, green beans, kidney beans, salt, pepper, and chicken stock. Bring to a boil, and simmer for at least 1 hour. Longer cooking will make the vegetables more tender and enhance the flavors, but 1 hour is the minimum cooking time.

4. If desired, fork-mash the vegetables before serving.

### 3 Servings

½ cup kidney beans, cooked
½ cup green beans
1 medium red potato, diced
1 medium carrot, diced
½ small onion, diced
1 tablespoon butter or margarine
dash of salt and pepper
4 cups chicken stock or water

**4 Servings**

*1 drumstick or thigh piece of
    chicken
6 cups of water
1 medium carrot, diced
1 small russet potato, diced
1 cup chicken broth
dash of salt and pepper
⅛ teaspoon dill
1 cup all-purpose flour
1 egg
¼ cup water*

# Chicken Stew with Dumplings

*Chicken stew is not a particularly fast recipe, but it's one that doesn't require
constant attention. The boiling and simmering stages can all go longer than
recommended; it will soften the veggies and increase the flavors.*

•   •   •   •   •

1.  Wash the chicken well, and remove the skin if desired. Bring to a boil
    in water. Simmer for 1–1½ hours, or until the meat begins falling off
    the bone.

2.  Remove the meat from the pot. Take off all the fat, skin, and bones.
    Shred the chicken into small pieces, and add back to the pot.

3.  Add potatoes and carrots to the chicken pot, along with the salt, pep-
    per, and dill. Simmer for 30–40 minutes, or until the vegetables are
    tender.

4.  Lightly beat the egg; add in the flour. Stir well, then add water 1 table-
    spoon at a time until a stiff dough is formed. Roll out the dough, then
    cut into small strips.

5.  Bring the chicken pot back to a boil. Add in the dumplings and broth,
    then simmer for an additional 40–45 minutes.

## Creamier Stew

*If your family prefers their stews on the creamy side (and no one has
an intolerance or allergy to dairy products), you can add a can of commercial cream of mushroom or cream of celery soup instead of the
broth to the stew during the last hour of simmering. In terms of just
thickening the stew, adding dumplings should do the job.*

# Bean Stew

*If your toddler's list of favorite foods doesn't include ground sausage, omit the meat from this recipe. Substitute with diced tomatoes or another type of legume, such as Great Northern or kidney beans.*

●　●　●　●　●

1. Cook the sausage in a medium saucepan, browning until it's completely cooked.

2. Drain the fat from the sausage, then add 2 cups of water and bring to a boil. Add the beans, carrot, and spices.

3. Simmer for 1½–2 hours.

### Hot Variation

*If your child has a penchant for spice, try using spicy sausage instead of its more benign cousin. For other family members who like their food spicier, you can add a little Tabasco to their bowl before serving. Don't assume that your toddler won't like spicy food—many toddlers actually prefer highly flavored foods by this age.*

**1 Serving**

½ cup white beans, cooked
¼ pound ground pork sausage
2 cups water, diced
1 medium carrot, diced
dash of paprika
dash of salt
dash of pepper
dash of oregano, crushed

## Turkey Noodle Soup

**4 Servings**

1 leftover turkey carcass
1 cup dried egg noodles
1 medium russet potato, diced
1 medium carrot, diced
1 stalk celery, diced
½ medium onion, diced
1 teaspoon salt
1 teaspoon pepper

*This classic recipe is good after Thanksgiving (it makes excellent use of the leftover turkey) but can be made just as easily by using chicken stock instead.*

• • • • •

1. Place the leftover turkey carcass, along with the salt and pepper, in a large saucepan and cover with water. Bring to a boil, and simmer for about 3 hours.

2. Strain the turkey stock. Tear the leftover turkey into shreds, discarding the fat and bones. Put 4 cups of stock in a medium saucepan; reserve the rest for another recipe.

3. Add potato, carrot, celery, and onion to the turkey stock. Bring to a boil; then reduce to a simmer. Simmer for 1 hour.

4. Add in the egg noodles and turkey meat, and simmer for another 45 minutes.

# Pork and Turnip Stew

*If you have fresh-picked turnips with the greens still intact, cook them along with the stew! They'll add extra flavor and vitamins. Wash well before cooking, and stay away from the shriveled shorter leaves—they're the most bitter.*

* * * * *

**3 Servings**

*6 ounces boneless pork roast*
*1 medium turnip, diced*
*1 medium carrot, diced*
*2 cups water*
*dash of garlic powder*
*1 tablespoon soy sauce*
*1 tablespoon butter*

1. Wash the pork, remove any fat, and cut into bite-size pieces. Melt the butter in a medium saucepan; brown the pork on all sides until completely cooked.

2. Add the water, carrot, garlic powder and soy sauce to the saucepan. Bring to a boil; then simmer for about 1½ hours.

3. Add the turnips to the saucepan, and simmer for 1 more hour, or until the meat and vegetables are tender.

4. Skim the surface of the stew to remove any fat before serving.

**Turnip Truths**

*Turnips, like potatoes, are root vegetables that are available year-round. They come in a range of sizes, though the smaller ones are likely to be sweeter and more suitable for toddler food. They're high in vitamin C, and are a fun new vegetable to incorporate into your toddler's diet.*

**1 Serving**

½ cup cauliflower
2 cups water
2 ounces cheese

# Cauliflower with Cheese

*Cauliflower may not be your favorite vegetable, but don't let that preju-
dice prevent you from serving it to your toddler. Serving it up with melted
cheese is a perfect way to encourage him to try a new taste.*

* * * * *

1. Wash the cauliflower, dice into small florets, and place in a steamer
   basket. Fill the bottom of a saucepan with water, place the steamer
   basket inside, then bring to a boil. Cook for 15 minutes, or until the
   cauliflower is tender.

2. Melt the cheese in a microwave-safe bowl. Heat in the microwave in
   30-second intervals, stirring in between, until well melted.

3. Place the cooked cauliflower in a bowl and pour the melted cheese
   on top.

### Glorious Leftovers
*Spicing up leftovers is a great way to serve a fresh new meal in no
time at all. Use whatever ingredients are on hand—mild spices,
melted cheese, diced ham—to turn any meal into something new and
delightful. It's easier and more convenient than cooking a whole new
meal from scratch every night, and you may stumble on some amazing
combinations.*

# Pasta and Broccoli

*Go as easy (or as heavy) on the garlic as your toddler seems to like.
You can easily use part of a clove, or an entire clove if she seems to
like it. This is also a perfect dish for serving to the rest of the family,
and it won't require any additional seasonings.*

●　●　●　●　●

**2 Servings**

*1 cup pasta*
*½ cup broccoli*
*½ clove garlic, minced*
*4 cups water*
*1 teaspoon olive oil*
*1 teaspoon grated Parmesan*
*1 teaspoon parsley*

1. Wash the broccoli and dice into small florets.

2. Bring the water to a boil. Add the pasta, and cook for about 10 minutes. Add in the broccoli and cook for another 10 minutes, or until both pasta and broccoli are tender. When cooked, drain.

3. Heat the olive oil in a medium skillet. Add garlic and parsley, sautéing for 2–3 minutes.

4. Add the pasta and broccoli to the saucepan. Sauté for 2–3 minutes, tossing the pasta and broccoli together with the garlic.

5. Sprinkle with Parmesan before serving.

## 2 Servings

½ cup spaghetti
2 cups water
¼ cup chicken or vegetable
   stock
1 tablespoon peanut butter
1 tablespoon soy sauce
½ teaspoon ginger, minced

# Peanut Butter Noodles

*This recipe is a fun Asian-based peanut sauce on top of plain old spaghetti. If your child has a peanut allergy, try substituting a nut butter made from sunflower seeds or pumpkin seeds.*

●　●　●　●　●

1. Bring the water to a boil. Add the spaghetti and cook for 15 minutes, or until the pasta is tender. Drain the noodles when they're cooked.

2. In a small saucepan, mix the stock, peanut butter, soy sauce, and ginger. Heat until peanut butter is just melted, stirring well.

3. Toss the noodles with the sauce.

4. For older children, serve with a small handful of chopped peanuts.

### Origins of Soy Sauce

*When soy sauce is made in the traditional way, soybeans are mixed with roasted wheat or rice and then fermented. After this process is complete (and it can take 2–3 months), the beans are drained and strained. The resulting liquid is soy sauce. Soybeans are an amazingly versatile legume!*

# Fluffy Lemon Pudding

*There are recipes for lemon pudding that don't involve baking, but most of them involve raw eggs. Try this one—it's a bit more work, but much safer for your toddler.*

* * * * *

**4 Servings**

*1 egg, separated*
*½ cup sugar*
*2 tablespoons all-purpose*
*    flour*
*3 tablespoons lemon juice*
*2 teaspoons lemon zest*
*½ cup milk (regular or soy)*
*dash salt*

1. Preheat oven to 350°F.

2. Place the egg yolk in a bowl. Beat in the sugar. Add in the flour, salt, and lemon zest. Stir in lemon juice and milk, and mix well.

3. In a separate bowl, whip the egg white to soft peaks using an electric mixer. Beat on high until when you lift one of the beaters out of the bowl, the egg whites form small white peaks. Fold the egg white into the rest of the batter.

4. Pour into a baking dish. Bake for 45 minutes, or until the pudding is set.

5. Let cool before serving, though adults may prefer the pudding warm. Store leftovers in the refrigerator.

¼ cup pearl tapioca
1½ cups milk
¼ cup sugar
1 egg
¼ teaspoon vanilla extract

# Tapioca

*If you're looking for an alternative to super-sweet store-bought puddings, try tapioca! It has a fun texture and a mild flavor that children will go for.*

⚫ ⚫ ⚫ ⚫ ⚫

1. Pour the milk into a small saucepan. Add the tapioca and bring almost to a boil.

2. Stir, and reduce the heat to a simmer. Cook for 6–7 minutes, stirring in the sugar as the tapioca simmers.

3. Beat the egg in a small bowl. Pour into the tapioca pot, and return almost to a boil.

4. Stirring constantly, reduce the heat, and simmer for an additional 8–10 minutes, or until the tapioca thickens up. Remove from heat and stir in the vanilla.

5. Allow to cool before serving.

### Tapioca

*Tapioca comes from the cassava root. Store-bought tapioca typically comes in pearls, small pellets that are cooked with milk to make a thick pudding. Tapioca itself is commonly used as a thickener in soups, stews, or pies. You may also find tapioca in pearl teas, hot or cold beverages with pearls of tapioca in the bottom.*

# Pear Pudding

*Here's an unusual pudding, made with fresh or canned pears, that provides a healthy snack or dessert for your toddler. If you like a crunchy topping on your pudding, try sprinkling graham cracker crumbs on top before baking.*

•   •   •   •   •

1. Preheat the oven to 375°F. Wash and peel the pear. Remove the stem and seeds, and grate the pear flesh.

2. Place the egg yolk in a bowl. Beat in lemon zest, cinnamon, and sugar. Mix in flour and milk; then stir in grated pear.

3. Whip the egg white to soft peaks using an electric mixer. Beat on high until, when you lift one of the beaters out of the bowl, the egg whites form small white peaks. Fold the egg white into the pear mixture.

4. Pour into a greased baking dish. Bake for about 30 minutes, or until pudding is set.

5. Allow to cool before serving.

## 2 Servings

1 medium pear
1 egg, separated
3 tablespoons all-purpose flour
2 tablespoons sugar
2 tablespoons milk (regular or soy)
1 teaspoon lemon zest
½ teaspoon cinnamon

# Banana Pudding

*While its chocolate and vanilla cousins are more readily available,
banana pudding is a fun dessert that any banana lover will enjoy.
Craving something that's more like Jell-O than pudding? Simply add a
packet of gelatin, adjusting the liquids as per the package directions.*

•   •   •   •   •

1. Whisk the egg in a small bowl. Beat in sugar.

2. Stir in the milk and cornstarch, mixing thoroughly.

3. Fork-mash the banana until it is completely creamed.

4. Pour the pudding mixture and banana into a small saucepan. Bring to a boil; then reduce the heat to medium. Stirring constantly, cook for 4–5 minutes, or until the pudding thickens.

5. Turn off the heat and stir in the vanilla. Mix well, and allow to cool before serving.

### Layer It Up
*A traditional way to serve banana pudding is a layered presentation in a glass or plastic bowl. Start with a layer of pudding, and follow with a layer of crushed vanilla wafer cookies. Add a layer of thinly sliced bananas, and another layer of pudding. Top it off with a dollop of whipped cream.*

# Chocolate Pudding

**2 Servings**

1 tablespoon butter
1 ounce unsweetened
    chocolate
1 cup milk
¼ cup flour
½ cup sugar
1 egg yolk
¼ teaspoon vanilla extract

*Ye Olde Standby. Chocolate pudding is as basic as it gets, and is
a favorite when all other mealtime foods turn into flops.*

* * * * *

1. Put the chocolate and butter into a microwave-safe dish. Microwave on low, in 30-second intervals, until the chocolate is melted. Stir well after each microwave interval to see if the chocolate is sufficiently melted.

2. Combine the melted chocolate and milk in a medium saucepan. Stir in the flour and sugar. Heat almost to boiling, and reduce heat to a simmer. Cook for 5–6 minutes, or until the pudding starts to gel together.

3. Give the pudding a good stir, and add the egg yolk. Stir well; then continue cooking over low heat for 2–3 minutes. Stir constantly to keep lumps from forming.

4. Remove the saucepan from the heat. Add in the vanilla and mix thoroughly.

5. Allow to cool before serving.

### Roll with the Pudding
*This is a good recipe for older children to practice their cooking skills with, but don't be too fussy about the end result! If it doesn't end up gelling into pudding, just call it hot chocolate. Toddlers can eat it with a spoon or drink it through a straw.*

## Vegetable Custard

**2 Servings**

¾ cup cooked carrots,
    potatoes, and peas
1 teaspoon butter or
    margarine
3 tablespoons milk (regular
    or soy)
2 teaspoons all-purpose
    flour or cornstarch
1 egg, beaten
1 tablespoon shredded
    Mozzarella

*For a pudding-like treat that you can feel good about serving, try this homemade
veggie custard. Feel free to substitute any leftover baked or grilled vegetables—
whatever is in season will be a nice addition.*

* * * * *

1. Preheat the oven to 350°F. Fork-mash the cooked vegetables.

2. Melt the butter in a saucepan. Add the milk and flour, and continue stirring over low heat until a thick sauce forms.

3. Over very low heat, stir the egg into the milk. Add the vegetables and cheese, mixing thoroughly to coat them in the sauce.

4. Pour the mixture into a small, greased dish. Bake for 35–40 minutes. It's done when a toothpick inserted into the middle of the custard comes out either clean or with just a few crumbs.

5. Allow to cool before serving.

# Vanilla Custard

*Vanilla custard is a soothing dish that is best served cold, so don't start this recipe 5 minutes before you plan to eat it! Refrigerate it for 2–3 hours before serving.*

· · · · ·

**1 Serving**

1 egg
2 tablespoons sugar
1 tablespoon cornstarch
½ cup milk (regular or soy)
¼ teaspoon vanilla extract

1. In a small bowl, whisk the egg together with the sugar. When mixed, stir in the cornstarch.

2. Add in vanilla and milk, stirring until they are completely combined.

3. Pour the mixture into a medium saucepan. Heat to scalding, reduce the heat to medium, and stir until the mixture thickens. Keep stirring, or the cornstarch is likely to become lumpy.

4. Once thick, pour the custard into a pan or small glass dish and cover it with plastic wrap. Refrigerate for several hours before serving.

## Vanilla Beans

*If you like your spices right from the source, try using vanilla beans instead of vanilla extract. Vanilla beans may be difficult to find in regular grocery stores, but they're inexpensive and highly flavorful. Replace a teaspoon of vanilla extract with about 1 inch of bean. Just make sure to remove the bean before serving!*

## 1 Serving

¼ cup semisweet chocolate
   chips
1 teaspoon butter
1 ripe banana
1 egg
2 tablespoons sugar
1 tablespoon cornstarch
½ cup milk (regular or soy)
¼ teaspoon vanilla extract

# Chocolate Banana Custard

*Chocolate and bananas make a fantastic combination, so this custard
should come as no surprise! If you find yourself with leftover melted chocolate, try coating a banana with it and freezing for a couple hours—frozen
bananas will win you some bonus points with the kids.*

* * * * *

1. Put the chocolate and butter into a microwave-safe dish. Microwave on low, in 30-second intervals, until the chocolate is melted. Stir well after each interval to see if the chocolate is sufficiently melted.

2. Fork-mash the banana until it is completely creamed.

3. In a small bowl, whisk the egg together with the sugar. When mixed, stir in the cornstarch.

4. Add vanilla and milk, stirring until they are completely combined. Pour in the melted chocolate and banana, stirring to combine.

5. Pour the mixture into a medium saucepan. Heat to scalding, reduce the heat to medium, and stir until the mixture thickens. Keep stirring, or the cornstarch is likely to become lumpy.

6. Once thick, pour the custard into a small heat-proof glass dish and cover it with plastic wrap. Refrigerate for several hours before serving.

# Coconut Egg Custard

*This type of custard is common in the Caribbean. While fresh coconut milk is as authentic as you can get, it may not be readily available. The canned variety is perfectly acceptable.*

●　●　●　●　●

**1 Serving**

*1 egg*
*2 tablespoons sugar*
*1 tablespoon cornstarch*
*¼ teaspoon vanilla extract*
*½ cup coconut milk*
*¼ cup milk (regular or soy)*
*¼ cup shredded coconut*

1. In a small bowl, whisk the egg together with the sugar. When mixed, stir in the cornstarch.

2. Add in the vanilla, coconut milk, and milk, stirring until they are completely combined. Stir in shredded coconut.

3. Pour the mixture into a medium saucepan. Heat to scalding, reduce the heat to medium, and stir until the mixture thickens. Keep stirring, or the cornstarch is likely to become lumpy.

4. Once thick, pour the custard into a small heat-proof glass dish and cover it with plastic wrap. Refrigerate for several hours before serving.

### A Sweeter Touch

*You can sweeten up any custard recipe by substituting half the milk with sweetened condensed milk. Because there's no soy-based version of condensed milk, you won't be able to make a non dairy version.*

**2 Servings**

¾ cup milk
¼ cup sugar
2 egg yolks
1 cup cream
½ teaspoon vanilla extract
8–10 cups ice cubes
1–2 cups rock salt

# Homemade Vanilla Ice Cream

*While ice cream is easy to make in an ice-cream maker, it's possible to do it your-self without any specialized equipment. Be prepared for a workout, though! You may need to enlist a friend with strong arm muscles.*

●　●　●　●　●

1. Heat the milk to scalding in a medium saucepan. Add in sugar, reduce the heat to medium, and stir until the sugar is dissolved. Add in egg yolks and stir for 1 minute.

2. Remove from heat when the mixture begins to thicken into custard. Pour in the cream and vanilla, stirring thoroughly to combine.

3. Pour into a small plastic container. Place this container inside a larger bowl. Fill the bowl with ice and salt so that your ice-cream container is surrounded on all sides.

4. Stir the ice cream constantly for about 15–20 minutes. When the ice cream starts feeling cold and thick (instead of warm and thin), it's getting close to being done. Continue stirring until it's thick enough to suit your tastes.

5. An alternative method is to pour the custard mixture into a sealing plastic baggie, then knead it inside the ice and salt bowl for 15 minutes. Wear gloves, or your hands will get very cold!

# Strawberry Ice Pops

**4 Servings**

1½ cups water
½ cup orange juice
4 large strawberries

*If you don't have plastic molds, try using disposable paper cups to make this summertime treat. Insert a popsicle stick once the pop is partially frozen; then simply peel off the cup when it's time to eat.*

* * * * *

1. Purée the strawberries in a food processor or blender.

2. Add water and orange juice to the food processor and mix until completely combined.

3. Pour into a rack of 4 ice-pop molds. Freeze for at least 5 hours before serving.

# Lemon Rice Pudding

**4 Servings**

½ cup rice
1 cup water
2 tablespoons milk or cream
1 teaspoon butter or
      margarine
1 egg
2 tablespoons brown sugar
1 tablespoon lemon juice
½ teaspoon lemon zest

*This pudding is not as creamy as some; rather, it offers a soft texture from the rice, mixed with the sweet-sour sensation of sugar and lemons.*

* * * * *

1. Bring the water, rice, and butter to a boil in a medium saucepan.

2. Reduce heat to a simmer, and stir in the cream. Once the rice returns to a simmer, cook for 25–30 minutes, or until the liquid is absorbed.

3. Turn down the heat to very low. Beat the egg and stir it into the rice pot.

4. Add in the lemon juice, lemon zest, and sugar. Mix thoroughly and continue to stir until the pudding thickens.

5. Remove from heat, and allow to cool before serving. Refrigerate the leftovers immediately.

**2 Servings**

1 cup blueberries
2 teaspoons white sugar
1 teaspoon brown sugar
1 tablespoon butter
¼ cup oatmeal

# Blueberry Crumble

*Fruit crumbles are simple desserts that go well with Homemade Vanilla Ice Cream (page 278) or whipped cream. It also goes nicely with Vanilla Custard (page 275).*

•  •  •  •  •

1. Preheat the oven to 350°F. Wash the blueberries. Place into a small baking dish. Mix the white sugar into the berries.

2. In a separate small dish, mash the butter, brown sugar, and oatmeal together with a fork.

3. When the mixture forms small crumbs, sprinkle over the top of the berries.

4. Bake for 30 minutes, or until the topping is brown and crunchy. Cool to room temperature before serving.

**8 Servings**

3 eggs
1 cup all-purpose flour
⅔ cup sugar
2 tablespoons melted butter
    or margarine

# Sponge Cake

*Here's a sweet treat for your toddler that is made from only four ingredients. It's quick to prepare and flavored simply enough to appeal to most children.*

•  •  •  •  •

1. Preheat the oven to 375°F.

2. Beat the eggs and sugar together in a medium bowl; mix until the eggs have a light, fluffy consistency. Add in the melted butter, stirring until it's thoroughly combined.

3. Mix in flour, and pour the batter into a greased 8-inch cake pan.

4. Bake for about 20–25 minutes, or until a toothpick inserted into the middle of the cake comes out clean. The cake should have a slightly springy consistency when the top is lightly pressed.

# Frozen Fruit

*Frozen fruit is an inexpensive summer treat that's quick to make. Remember to remove all pits, stems, leaves, cores, and other inedibles before freezing!*

* * * * *

**1 Serving**
*4 grapes*
*1 strawberry*
*½ banana*

1. Wash the grapes and slice in half. Wash the strawberry, remove the hull, and slice into quarters. Peel the banana and slice into coins.

2. Place the fruit in a disposable paper cup.

3. Freeze for at least 4 hours before serving.

## Party Tips
*Frozen fruit is great for a summer birthday party. To make this simple dessert a little more festive, freeze the fruit in printed paper muffin cups or in decorated snack-sized zipper baggies. For added color, try using both red and green grapes, pineapple, and maraschino cherries. You can even add some watermelon, cantaloupe, or honeydew to produce a rainbow effect.*

**4 Servings**

1 cup water
½ cup heavy whipping
    cream
1 peach, diced

# Creamy Fruit Popsicles

*Not sure you want your child having all the additives commonly found in creamy popsicles? Make your own! While you can substitute soy milk for cream in this recipe, it doesn't freeze as well, so the end result will be a little icier than a dairy popsicle.*

● ● ● ● ●

1. Place the peach in a food processor or blender. Purée completely.

2. Add in the water and cream. Continue puréeing until the mixture is smooth.

3. Pour into a rack of 4 ice-pop molds. Freeze for at least 5 hours before serving.

### Substituting with Canned
*While canned peaches don't cut it for every recipe, they actually work just fine when making creamy popsicles. If you use the kind that are canned in syrup, the popsicles will come out a bit sweeter. You can even use the canning syrup instead of some of the water in this recipe.*

# Apple Nut Bake

*Here's an easy recipe that makes good use of leftover apples. Any variety will do. If using Granny Smiths, you may want to add a pinch more sugar. If your apples are already sweet enough, feel free to omit the sugar entirely.*

* * * * *

1. Preheat the oven to 350°F. Wash, peel, and core the apples. Dice into chunks.

2. Bring the water to a boil in a medium saucepan. Add the apple chunks and cook for 20–25 minutes, or until the apples are tender. Drain the apples and fork-mash into a rough purée.

3. Place the almonds in a food processor or food mill. Grind until they are finely chopped.

4. Mix the apples, almonds, and egg together in a bowl. Add the flour and sugar, stirring to combine. Add nutmeg and cinnamon, and stir until the mixture is thoroughly coated.

5. Place in a greased baking dish and bake for 30 minutes. Allow to cool before serving.

## 2 Servings

*2 medium apples*
*4 cups water*
*1 tablespoon almonds*
*1 egg*
*1 teaspoon sugar*
*1 teaspoon all-purpose flour*
*dash of cinnamon*
*dash of nutmeg*

½ cup crushed graham
   crackers
3 ounces semisweet
   chocolate
1 tablespoon shortening
1 cup powdered sugar
½ cup peanut butter
¼ cup chocolate chips

# Peanut Butter Goodies

*Peanut butter and chocolate is a devilishly delicious combination—treat your child's sweet tooth with this no-bake recipe. For variety, try substituting peanut butter chips or butterscotch chips for the chocolate.*

* * * * *

1. Place the graham crackers in a sealing plastic bag. Crush with your hands or a mallet to make coarse crumbs (this is a great task for toddlers).

2. Put the chocolate and shortening into a microwave-safe dish. Microwave on low, in 30-second intervals, until the chocolate is melted. Stir well after each microwave interval to see if the chocolate is sufficiently melted.

3. Mix the chocolate and sugar together until they're combined. Stir in peanut butter.

4. Add graham cracker crumbs. Mix gently until they are completely incorporated. Add chocolate chips and stir until thoroughly mixed.

5. Press into a loaf pan; then cut into cookies about 1" x 2".

### Making Parents Feel Better
*If the thought of gooey treats makes you want to run for the toothpaste, you can mitigate the health concerns by adding a tablespoon of wheat germ to these peanut butter goodies. Also, instead of chocolate chips, try throwing in a few "twigs" of an oat bran cereal.*

# Lentil Stew

*Lentil stew is a healthy meal that requires little attention on the part of the chef. Once it's simmering, you can leave it alone for 2–3 hours.*

* * * * *

1. Bring water to a boil. Add the lentils, tomato, celery, and garlic.

2. Simmer for 2½–3 hours.

**1 Serving**

*½ cup lentils*
*2 cups water*
*¼ teaspoon garlic powder*
*½ celery stalk, diced*
*1 plum tomato, diced*

# Macaroni Salad

*Don't eat the warmed-over picnic macaroni salad—make your own from scratch! Use leftover cooked macaroni to speed up the preparation time.*

* * * * *

1. Dice the pickle into very small pieces, and mix with the macaroni.

2. Mix in the mayonnaise.

3. Toss with the onion powder and pepper.

**1 Serving**

*½ cup cooked macaroni*
*1 tablespoon mayonnaise*
*½ small pickle*
*dash of pepper*
*dash of onion powder*

*2 fresh apricots*
*¼ cup vanilla yogurt*
*1 teaspoon orange juice*
*1 teaspoon apricot nectar,*
*    optional*

# Creamy Apricots

*Apricots are great by themselves, but can be made even better*
*when teased into a creamy dessert. For an extra-rich treat, use*
*melted vanilla ice cream instead of yogurt.*

●　●　●　●　●

1. Wash the apricots. Remove the pits, and dice into small pieces.

2. Stir the yogurt, nectar, and orange juice together in a small bowl. Pour over the apricots.

3. Fork-mash together. Serve chilled.

### Super-Creamed Apricots

*A nice variation on this recipe is Apricot Cream. Combine the apricots with a teaspoon of sugar, cover with water in a small saucepan, and cook until the apricots are very soft (about 15 minutes). Drain, purée in the food processor, and return to a small saucepan. Add a tablespoon of cream and cook over low heat until the mixture forms a delightfully smooth sauce. Serve over fresh fruit.*

# Peach and Grape Gelatin

*Don't want to wait several hours for your gelatin dessert? Try cooking it using the quick-set method. Boil ½ cup of water to mix into the gelatin. Once dissolved, add in ½ cup of cold water and 1 cup ice cubes. With this method, you'll only need to refrigerate it for 1 hour or less.*

• • • • •

1. Wash the peach; remove the skin and pit. Dice into small pieces.

2. Wash the grapes and slice in half.

3. Bring 1 cup of water to a boil in a medium saucepan. Stir in gelatin mix and cook until completely dissolved.

4. Remove from heat. Stir in 1 cup cold water and the diced fruit.

5. Pour into a lightly greased gelatin mold or dish. Refrigerate until set, 3–4 hours.

## 6 Servings

1 small package (3 ounces) peach-flavored gelatin mix
½ cup grapes
½ ripe peach
2 cups water

½ cup heavy whipping
 cream
3 ounces cream cheese
¼ cup sugar
½ cup strawberries
¼ cup blueberries
¼ cup peaches
¼ cup honeydew or
 cantaloupe
¼ cup grapes

# Fruit Parfait

*A parfait is a fun summery dessert that is suitable for toddlers, older children, grownups, and guests alike. This recipe omits a crunchy topping that may be unsuitable for young eaters, but feel free to top it with baked oats or granola.*

•  •  •  •  •

1. Wash all the fruit. Remove any stems or seeds, then dice into small pieces.

2. Whip the whipping cream using an electric mixer. Alternatively, use 1 cup of whipped regular or non-dairy topping.

3. Mix the cream cheese and sugar together in a small bowl. Gently stir in the whipped cream.

4. In a transparent plastic cup, place a 1-inch layer of fruit. Follow with a 1-inch layer of cream cheese. Repeat until fruit and cheese are used. This recipe should make 2 medium cups.

### Creamy Parfait

*Prepare a packet of berry-flavored gelatin according to the package directions. After it has solidified in the refrigerator, mix it with an equal amount of whipped cream. Use this cream as an alternating layer with fruit, and presto! Parfait magic.*

# Apple-Apricot Roll

*This delicious treat is sure to please your taste buds along with your toddler's! You can also omit the dough and purée the fruit for younger toddlers, or fork-mash it for those who just need a little help.*

* * * * *

1. Preheat the oven to 375°F. Wash and peel the apple. Remove the core and dice into chunks. Remove the pits from the apricots, and dice into chunks.

2. Bring a cup of water to a boil. Add the fruit and 1 tablespoon sugar. Reduce to a simmer, and cook for about 15 minutes, or until the fruit is tender. Drain most of the liquid; then fork-mash into a lumpy purée

3. Mix the butter and sugar to form large crumbs. Stir in the egg and vanilla. Once mixed, add flour, salt, and baking soda. Mix until a stiff dough is formed.

4. Roll the dough out on a floured work surface to about ⅛-inch thickness. Fill half of the dough with the cooked fruit, fold the dough over, and pinch the edges together to seal. Sprinkle the top with rock sugar.

5. Bake in a greased dish for 15 minutes, or until the dough is lightly browned. Allow to cool, and slice into ¼-inch thick cookies.

## 8 Servings

1 medium apple
3 apricots
2 tablespoons sugar
1 cup water
2 tablespoons butter or margarine
1 cup all-purpose flour
1 egg
¼ teaspoon baking soda
¼ teaspoon salt
½ teaspoon vanilla extract
1 tablespoon rock sugar, optional

# Fruit Tofu Dessert

**2 Servings**

2 large strawberries
1 apricot
½ ripe peach
1 cup water
¼ cup soy yogurt
½ cup silken tofu

*Soy-based desserts are a healthy alternative to treats with cream or butter. They're also highly satisfying, and introduce new tastes and textures into your toddler's diet. Try offering your child the leftover tofu for a snack; simply dice into cubes.*

●　●　●　●　●

1. Wash the strawberries and remove the hulls. Slice in half. Wash the apricot and peach. Peel them, remove the pits, and cut into chunks.

2. Place the apricot, peach, and strawberries in a small saucepan with 1 cup water. Bring to a boil, and simmer for 10–15 minutes or until the fruit is tender. Drain the fruit.

3. Combine the tofu and yogurt in a food processor or blender. Purée until they are creamed together.

4. Stir them into the fruit. Either fork-mash together, serve the tofu cream over the fruit, or purée together in the food processor.

### Is Soy Yogurt Completely Nondairy?
*Unless otherwise marked on the package, soy yogurt is completely nondairy. Soy yogurt is made from soy milk and generally contains no whey or other dairy products. Soy yogurt is no longer a specialty, hard-to-find item; it's often sold in mainstream grocery stores, usually in the refrigerated organic section.*

# Creamy Fruit Gelatin

*Most children like the wobble factor in gelatin desserts, but some may prefer a creamier, milkier taste that you can achieve using this recipe. Be sure to refrigerate the leftovers promptly with this recipe.*

* * * * *

1. Peel the orange. Divide into sections, remove as much of the white skin as possible, and dice into small pieces.

2. Bring 1 cup of water to a boil in a medium saucepan. Stir in the gelatin and cook until completely dissolved. Remove from the heat.

3. Stir the cream cheese to soften it, and mix it into the hot gelatin. Stir until the cream cheese is completely dissolved.

4. Whip the whipping cream using an electric mixer. Alternatively, use 1 cup of whipped regular or nondairy topping. Stir into the gelatin mixture, mixing well. Add in the orange pieces and stir to mix.

5. Pour into a lightly greased gelatin mold or dish. Refrigerate until set, about 5–6 hours.

**4 Servings**

1 small package (3 ounces) lemon-flavored gelatin mix
1 small package (3 ounces) unflavored gelatin
1 orange
2 cups water
1 small package (8 ounces) cream cheese
¼ cup heavy whipping cream

Appendix **A**

# Food Introduction Tips

Contradictory to folklore or what you may read in parenting magazines, there is no hard-and-fast rule as to which foods to introduce to your baby first. Many people are convinced that rice should be introduced first. Breastfed babies, however, are already getting plenty of carbohydrates, so meats (high in protein) may make a good first choice.

Worried your baby will develop a sweet tooth if you give her bananas before beans? Don't fret! There's no evidence that first foods influence future food choices to that degree. The following list can serve as a guideline for introducing foods by age, but talk to your doctor and together you can make the best decisions for your baby.

### 4–6 Months

**Breastmilk or iron-fortified infant formula:** maintain your baby's primary form of liquid nutrition at least throughout the first year.

**Iron-fortified rice cereal:** a common first food because it isn't likely to be allergenic, and contains the additional iron that breastfed babies will need starting at around 6 months. Also, try whole-grain oatmeal and barley cereal.

**Single puréed vegetables:** squash, green beans, sweet potatoes. Choose vegetables with a mild flavor and serve them individually. Don't offer combined vegetable-and-meat meals until your baby has proven not to be allergic to any of the components.

**Single puréed or mashed fruits:** apple, peach, banana.

If you have a family history of food allergies, you may want to delay starting solid foods to at least 6 months and perhaps as long as 9 months. Look for signs of readiness, such as them watching you eat and trying to grab bits of food from you.

Also, be sure to serve cereals with a spoon and never in a baby bottle. Mix with either breastmilk, water, or formula. Make the mixture initially very thin; then make it thicker (by adding less liquid) as your baby gets older and more confident with spoon-feeding. Expose your baby to warm and cold cereal.

### 6–9 Months

**Single puréed meats:** chicken, beef, turkey.

**Combination vegetable purées with minimal texture:** Fork-mash very soft vegetables.

**More "exotic" puréed fruits:** mango, papaya, cantaloupe.

### 9–12 Months

**Egg yolks:** well-cooked yolks can be served after your baby has a proven tolerance for meats, or at around 9 months. Wait until after a year to introduce egg whites.

**Cheeses:** offer Cheddar, Mozzarella, and other mild cheeses. Avoid blue cheese, Brie, and other soft cheeses until your baby is at least a year old.

**Finger foods for teething:** biter biscuits, graham crackers, teething biscotti, teething rusks. Go for recipes with few ingredients, and watch for signs of a wheat allergy.

**Yogurt:** offer in small amounts until your baby has proven that she doesn't have a dairy allergy.

**Tofu:** serve cubes of soft (silken) tofu for self-feeding.

### 12–18 Months:

**Egg whites:** these may cause an allergic reaction, so never serve before 12 months.

**Honey:** because of a risk of botulism, never serve before 12 months.

**Cow's milk:** due to high allergenic potential and digestive issues, hold off on cow's milk until at least 12 months. Also hold off as a substitute for breastmilk or formula because cow's milk doesn't have iron in it.

**Citrus fruits:** oranges, grapefruit, lemons. Withhold these until 12 months, because they cause an allergic reaction in some children.

**Pasta:** spaghetti, rotini, other fun shapes. Cook well, and supervise your baby while she is eating them.

**Protein:** beans, lentils. Go easy on the amounts, because too much fiber can lead to diarrhea. Offer cooked meats and mixed vegetables with pasta, such as chicken and rice or beef noodle stew.

### 18–24 Months:

**Raw fruits and vegetables:** cut pieces small enough that they can be swallowed without chewing, just in case! Make sure all fruits and vegetables are scrubbed or peeled before serving.

### 24–36 Months:

Your baby can have most foods by this time, but now you can prepare him for a lifetime of healthy eating. Offer foods from all categories of the pyramid, and give him meals that require a plate, fork, and spoon.

# Nutritional Information for Common Baby Foods

The number of calories that a baby or toddler needs to stay healthy depends on your child's individual metabolism, how active she is, and how quickly she is growing. In general, you can figure out how many calories per day your child should be eating based on either her weight (for less than 12 months) or her height (for ages 1–3 years).

For infants, the basic calorie requirement is about 50 calories per pound. Of course, if your baby is growing particularly fast, he might need more food—some babies need as few as 35 calories per pound or as many as 75 calories per pound. As long as his height and weight are increasing and are following his particular curve on a growth chart, you don't need to worry. Remember that breastmilk or iron-fortified formula will remain your child's primary source of nutrition in his first year—solid foods are just a supplement.

The phenomenal growth of your baby's first year will slow down once she hits the toddler years, and her calorie requirements also begin to slow down. The average toddler needs about 40 calories per day for every inch of height. In addition to calories, your child will also need the required amounts of other vitamins and minerals to stay healthy. Providing a multi-vitamin is certainly an option, but most vitamins are absorbed best from natural sources. The following list details twhe vitamins and other nutrients found in a number of fruits, vegetables, and other foods liked by many babies. Experiment and find your child's favorites!

### Acorn Squash
Typical serving size . . . . . . . . . . . . . . . . . . . . . . . . . . . . . . . ½ cup
Calories. . . . . . . . . . . . . . . . . . . . . . . . . . . . . . . . . . . . . . . . 75
Potassium . . . . . . . . . . . . . . . . . . . . . . . . . . . . . . . . . . . . .450 mg
Vitamin A . . . . . . . . . . . . . . . . . . . . . . . . . . . . . . . . . . . 450 IU
Vitamin C . . . . . . . . . . . . . . . . . . . . . . . . . . . . . . . . . . . .12 mg
Dietary Fiber. . . . . . . . . . . . . . . . . . . . . . . . . . . . . . . . . . .3.2 g

### Apples
Typical serving size . . . . . . . . . . . . . . . . . . . . . . . . . . . . . .½ medium
Calories. . . . . . . . . . . . . . . . . . . . . . . . . . . . . . . . . . . . . . . .50
Potassium . . . . . . . . . . . . . . . . . . . . . . . . . . . . . . . . . . . . .79 mg
Vitamin A . . . . . . . . . . . . . . . . . . . . . . . . . . . . . . . . . . . . 37 IU
Vitamin C . . . . . . . . . . . . . . . . . . . . . . . . . . . . . . . . . . . . .3 mg
Dietary Fiber. . . . . . . . . . . . . . . . . . . . . . . . . . . . . . . . . . . 1.7 g

### Avocados
Typical serving size . . . . . . . . . . . . . . . . . . . . . . . . . . . . . . .¼ cup
Calories. . . . . . . . . . . . . . . . . . . . . . . . . . . . . . . . . . . . . . . .60

Potassium . . . . . . . . . . . . . . . . . . . . . . . . . . . . . . . . . . . . . . . 110 mg
Vitamin A . . . . . . . . . . . . . . . . . . . . . . . . . . . . . . . . . . . . 25 IU
Vitamin C . . . . . . . . . . . . . . . . . . . . . . . . . . . . . . . . . . . . . .1 mg
Dietary Fiber. . . . . . . . . . . . . . . . . . . . . . . . . . . . . . . . . . . .1.8 g

**Brown Rice**
Serving size . . . . . . . . . . . . . . . . . . . . . . . . . . . . . . . . . ⅛ cup dry
Calories. . . . . . . . . . . . . . . . . . . . . . . . . . . . . . . . . . . . . . . .85
Potassium . . . . . . . . . . . . . . . . . . . . . . . . . . . . . . . . . . . . . .50 mg
Vitamin A . . . . . . . . . . . . . . . . . . . . . . . . . . . . . . . . . . . . . . .0
Vitamin C . . . . . . . . . . . . . . . . . . . . . . . . . . . . . . . . . . . . . . .0
Dietary Fiber. . . . . . . . . . . . . . . . . . . . . . . . . . . . . . . . . . . 1 g

**Carrots**
Typical serving size . . . . . . . . . . . . . . . . . . . . . . . . .¼ cup cooked
Calories. . . . . . . . . . . . . . . . . . . . . . . . . . . . . . . . . . . . . . . 15
Potassium . . . . . . . . . . . . . . . . . . . . . . . . . . . . . . . . . . . . . 115 mg
Vitamin A . . . . . . . . . . . . . . . . . . . . . . . . . . . . . . . . . . 7350 IU
Vitamin C . . . . . . . . . . . . . . . . . . . . . . . . . . . . . . . . . . . . .6 mg
Dietary Fiber. . . . . . . . . . . . . . . . . . . . . . . . . . . . . . . . . . .1.5 g

**Corn**
Typical serving size . . . . . . . . . . . . . . . . . . . . . . . . . . . . .¼ cup
Calories. . . . . . . . . . . . . . . . . . . . . . . . . . . . . . . . . . . . . . . .45
Potassium . . . . . . . . . . . . . . . . . . . . . . . . . . . . . . . . . . . . . 115 mg
Vitamin A . . . . . . . . . . . . . . . . . . . . . . . . . . . . . . . . . . . 1 IU
Vitamin C . . . . . . . . . . . . . . . . . . . . . . . . . . . . . . . . . . . . .3 mg
Dietary Fiber. . . . . . . . . . . . . . . . . . . . . . . . . . . . . . . . . . .1.1 g

**Green Beans**
Typical serving size . . . . . . . . . . . . . . . . . . . . . . . . .¼ cup cooked
Calories. . . . . . . . . . . . . . . . . . . . . . . . . . . . . . . . . . . . . . . 12
Potassium . . . . . . . . . . . . . . . . . . . . . . . . . . . . . . . . . . . . . .65 mg
Vitamin A . . . . . . . . . . . . . . . . . . . . . . . . . . . . . . . . . . 200 IU
Vitamin C . . . . . . . . . . . . . . . . . . . . . . . . . . . . . . . . . . . . .3 mg
Dietary Fiber. . . . . . . . . . . . . . . . . . . . . . . . . . . . . . . . . . 1 g

## Oatmeal

Typical serving size . . . . . . . . . . . . . . . . . . . . . . . . . . . . . ¼ cup dry
Calories. . . . . . . . . . . . . . . . . . . . . . . . . . . . . . . . . . . . . . . . .60
Potassium . . . . . . . . . . . . . . . . . . . . . . . . . . . . . . . . . . . . . . . .50
Vitamin A . . . . . . . . . . . . . . . . . . . . . . . . . . . . . . . . . . . . . . . . .0
Vitamin C . . . . . . . . . . . . . . . . . . . . . . . . . . . . . . . . . . . . . . . . .0
Dietary Fiber. . . . . . . . . . . . . . . . . . . . . . . . . . . . . . . . . . . . . . 1 g

## Pasta, Enriched

Typical serving size . . . . . . . . . . . . . . . . . . . . . . . . . . . . . ⅛ cup dry
Calories. . . . . . . . . . . . . . . . . . . . . . . . . . . . . . . . . . . . . . . . .55
Potassium . . . . . . . . . . . . . . . . . . . . . . . . . . . . . . . . . . . . . . . . .0
Vitamin A . . . . . . . . . . . . . . . . . . . . . . . . . . . . . . . . . . . . . . . . .0
Vitamin C . . . . . . . . . . . . . . . . . . . . . . . . . . . . . . . . . . . . . . . . .0
Dietary Fiber. . . . . . . . . . . . . . . . . . . . . . . . . . . . . . . . . . . . .0.5 g

## Peaches

Typical serving size . . . . . . . . . . . . . . . . . . . . . . . . . . . . . ½ medium
Calories. . . . . . . . . . . . . . . . . . . . . . . . . . . . . . . . . . . . . . . . .25
Potassium . . . . . . . . . . . . . . . . . . . . . . . . . . . . . . . . . . . . . .94 mg
Vitamin A . . . . . . . . . . . . . . . . . . . . . . . . . . . . . . . . . . . . 100 IU
Vitamin C . . . . . . . . . . . . . . . . . . . . . . . . . . . . . . . . . . . . . .4 mg
Dietary Fiber. . . . . . . . . . . . . . . . . . . . . . . . . . . . . . . . . . . . . . 1 g

## Pearl Barley

Typical serving size . . . . . . . . . . . . . . . . . . . . . . . . . . . . . ⅛ cup dry
Calories. . . . . . . . . . . . . . . . . . . . . . . . . . . . . . . . . . . . . . . . .90
Potassium . . . . . . . . . . . . . . . . . . . . . . . . . . . . . . . . . . . . . .36 mg
Vitamin A . . . . . . . . . . . . . . . . . . . . . . . . . . . . . . . . . . . . . . . . .0
Vitamin C . . . . . . . . . . . . . . . . . . . . . . . . . . . . . . . . . . . . . . . . .0
Dietary Fiber. . . . . . . . . . . . . . . . . . . . . . . . . . . . . . . . . . 4 grams

## Pears

Typical serving size . . . . . . . . . . . . . . . . . . . . . . . . . . . . . ½ medium
Calories. . . . . . . . . . . . . . . . . . . . . . . . . . . . . . . . . . . . . . . . .48

Potassium . . . . . . . . . . . . . . . . . . . . . . . . . . . . . . . . . . . . . . . . .100 mg
Vitamin A . . . . . . . . . . . . . . . . . . . . . . . . . . . . . . . . . . . . . . . . 23 IU
Vitamin C . . . . . . . . . . . . . . . . . . . . . . . . . . . . . . . . . . . . . . . . .3 mg
Dietary Fiber. . . . . . . . . . . . . . . . . . . . . . . . . . . . . . . . . . . . . . .2.5 g

**Peas**
Typical serving size . . . . . . . . . . . . . . . . . . . . . . . . . . .¼ cup cooked
Calories. . . . . . . . . . . . . . . . . . . . . . . . . . . . . . . . . . . . . . . . . . 11
Potassium . . . . . . . . . . . . . . . . . . . . . . . . . . . . . . . . . . . . . . . . .45 mg
Vitamin A . . . . . . . . . . . . . . . . . . . . . . . . . . . . . . . . . . . . . . 500 IU
Vitamin C . . . . . . . . . . . . . . . . . . . . . . . . . . . . . . . . . . . . . . . . .21 mg
Dietary Fiber. . . . . . . . . . . . . . . . . . . . . . . . . . . . . . . . . . . . . . 1.3 g

**Plums**
Typical serving size . . . . . . . . . . . . . . . . . . . . . . . . . . . . . .½ medium
Calories. . . . . . . . . . . . . . . . . . . . . . . . . . . . . . . . . . . . . . . . . .20
Potassium . . . . . . . . . . . . . . . . . . . . . . . . . . . . . . . . . . . . . . . . .90 mg
Vitamin A . . . . . . . . . . . . . . . . . . . . . . . . . . . . . . . . . . . . . . 350 IU
Vitamin C . . . . . . . . . . . . . . . . . . . . . . . . . . . . . . . . . . . . . . . . .4 mg
Dietary Fiber. . . . . . . . . . . . . . . . . . . . . . . . . . . . . . . . . . . . . . 1 g

**Spinach**
Typical serving size . . . . . . . . . . . . . . . . . . . . . . . . . . . . . . . .¼ cup
Calories. . . . . . . . . . . . . . . . . . . . . . . . . . . . . . . . . . . . . . . . . 12
Potassium . . . . . . . . . . . . . . . . . . . . . . . . . . . . . . . . . . . . . . . .248 mg
Vitamin A . . . . . . . . . . . . . . . . . . . . . . . . . . . . . . . . . . . . . . .4710 IU
Vitamin C . . . . . . . . . . . . . . . . . . . . . . . . . . . . . . . . . . . . . . . . .4 mg
Dietary Fiber. . . . . . . . . . . . . . . . . . . . . . . . . . . . . . . . . . . . . . 1.1 g

**Sweet Potatoes**
Typical serving size . . . . . . . . . . . . . . . . . . . . . . . . . . . . . . . .¼ cup
Calories. . . . . . . . . . . . . . . . . . . . . . . . . . . . . . . . . . . . . . . . . .45
Potassium . . . . . . . . . . . . . . . . . . . . . . . . . . . . . . . . . . . . . . . .190 mg
Vitamin A . . . . . . . . . . . . . . . . . . . . . . . . . . . . . . . . . . . . . . .8100 IU
Vitamin C . . . . . . . . . . . . . . . . . . . . . . . . . . . . . . . . . . . . . . 6.1 mg
Dietary Fiber. . . . . . . . . . . . . . . . . . . . . . . . . . . . . . . . . . . . . . 1.8 g

# Index

# The EVERYTHING Series!

## BUSINESS & PERSONAL FINANCE

Everything® **Accounting Book**
Everything® Budgeting Book
Everything® Business Planning Book
Everything® Coaching and Mentoring Book
Everything® Fundraising Book
Everything® Get Out of Debt Book
Everything® Grant Writing Book
Everything® Home-Based Business Book, 2nd Ed.
Everything® Homebuying Book, 2nd Ed.
Everything® Homeselling Book, 2nd Ed.
Everything® Investing Book, 2nd Ed.
Everything® Landlording Book
Everything® Leadership Book
Everything® **Managing People Book, 2nd Ed.**
Everything® Negotiating Book
Everything® Online Auctions Book
Everything® Online Business Book
Everything® Personal Finance Book
Everything® Personal Finance in Your 20s and 30s Book
Everything® Project Management Book
Everything® Real Estate Investing Book
Everything® Robert's Rules Book, $7.95
Everything® Selling Book
Everything® **Start Your Own Business Book, 2nd Ed.**
Everything® Wills & Estate Planning Book

## COOKING

Everything® Barbecue Cookbook
Everything® Bartender's Book, $9.95
Everything® Chinese Cookbook
Everything® **Classic Recipes Book**
Everything® Cocktail Parties and Drinks Book
Everything® College Cookbook
Everything® **Cooking for Baby and Toddler Book**
Everything® Cooking for Two Cookbook
Everything® Diabetes Cookbook
Everything® Easy Gourmet Cookbook
Everything® Fondue Cookbook
Everything® **Fondue Party Book**
Everything® Gluten-Free Cookbook
Everything® Glycemic Index Cookbook
Everything® Grilling Cookbook

Everything® Healthy Meals in Minutes Cookbook
Everything® Holiday Cookbook
Everything® Indian Cookbook
Everything® Italian Cookbook
Everything® Low-Carb Cookbook
Everything® Low-Fat High-Flavor Cookbook
Everything® Low-Salt Cookbook
Everything® Meals for a Month Cookbook
Everything® Mediterranean Cookbook
Everything® Mexican Cookbook
Everything® One-Pot Cookbook
Everything® **Quick and Easy 30-Minute, 5-Ingredient Cookbook**
Everything® Quick Meals Cookbook
Everything® Slow Cooker Cookbook
Everything® Slow Cooking for a Crowd Cookbook
Everything® Soup Cookbook
Everything® Tex-Mex Cookbook
Everything® Thai Cookbook
Everything® Vegetarian Cookbook
Everything® Wild Game Cookbook
Everything® Wine Book, 2nd Ed.

## GAMES

Everything® 15-Minute Sudoku Book, $9.95
Everything® 30-Minute Sudoku Book, $9.95
Everything® Blackjack Strategy Book
Everything® Brain Strain Book, $9.95
Everything® Bridge Book
Everything® Card Games Book
Everything® Card Tricks Book, $9.95
Everything® Casino Gambling Book, 2nd Ed.
Everything® Chess Basics Book
Everything® Craps Strategy Book
Everything® Crossword and Puzzle Book
Everything® Crossword Challenge Book
Everything® Cryptograms Book, $9.95
Everything® Easy Crosswords Book
Everything® Easy Kakuro Book, $9.95
Everything® Games Book, 2nd Ed.
Everything® Giant Sudoku Book, $9.95
Everything® Kakuro Challenge Book, $9.95
Everything® **Large-Print Crossword Challenge Book**
Everything® Large-Print Crosswords Book
Everything® Lateral Thinking Puzzles Book, $9.95
Everything® **Mazes Book**

Everything® Pencil Puzzles Book, $9.95
Everything® Poker Strategy Book
Everything® Pool & Billiards Book
Everything® Test Your IQ Book, $9.95
Everything® Texas Hold 'Em Book, $9.95
Everything® Travel Crosswords Book, $9.95
Everything® Word Games Challenge Book
Everything® Word Search Book

## HEALTH

Everything® Alzheimer's Book
Everything® Diabetes Book
Everything® Health Guide to Adult Bipolar Disorder
Everything® Health Guide to Controlling Anxiety
Everything® Health Guide to Fibromyalgia
Everything® **Health Guide to Thyroid Disease**
Everything® Hypnosis Book
Everything® Low Cholesterol Book
Everything® Massage Book
Everything® Menopause Book
Everything® Nutrition Book
Everything® Reflexology Book
Everything® Stress Management Book

## HISTORY

Everything® American Government Book
Everything® American History Book
Everything® Civil War Book
Everything® Freemasons Book
Everything® Irish History & Heritage Book
Everything® Middle East Book

## HOBBIES

Everything® Candlemaking Book
Everything® Cartooning Book
Everything® **Coin Collecting Book**
Everything® Drawing Book
Everything® Family Tree Book, 2nd Ed.
Everything® Knitting Book
Everything® Knots Book
Everything® Photography Book
Everything® Quilting Book
Everything® Scrapbooking Book
Everything® Sewing Book
Everything® Woodworking Book

Bolded titles are new additions to the series.
All Everything® books are priced at $12.95 or $14.95, unless otherwise stated. Prices subject to change without notice.

## HOME IMPROVEMENT

Everything® Feng Shui Book
Everything® Feng Shui Decluttering Book, $9.95
Everything® Fix-It Book
Everything® Home Decorating Book
**Everything® Home Storage Solutions Book**
Everything® Homebuilding Book
Everything® Lawn Care Book
Everything® Organize Your Home Book

## KIDS' BOOKS

### All titles are $7.95

Everything® Kids' Animal Puzzle & Activity Book
Everything® Kids' Baseball Book, 4th Ed.
Everything® Kids' Bible Trivia Book
Everything® Kids' Bugs Book
**Everything® Kids' Cars and Trucks Puzzle & Activity Book**
Everything® Kids' Christmas Puzzle & Activity Book
Everything® Kids' Cookbook
Everything® Kids' Crazy Puzzles Book
Everything® Kids' Dinosaurs Book
**Everything® Kids' First Spanish Puzzle and Activity Book**
Everything® Kids' Gross Hidden Pictures Book
Everything® Kids' Gross Jokes Book
Everything® Kids' Gross Mazes Book
Everything® Kids' Gross Puzzle and Activity Book
Everything® Kids' Halloween Puzzle & Activity Book
Everything® Kids' Hidden Pictures Book
Everything® Kids' Horses Book
Everything® Kids' Joke Book
Everything® Kids' Knock Knock Book
**Everything® Kids' Learning Spanish Book**
Everything® Kids' Math Puzzles Book
Everything® Kids' Mazes Book
Everything® Kids' Money Book
Everything® Kids' Nature Book
Everything® Kids' Pirates Puzzle and Activity Book
**Everything® Kids' Princess Puzzle and Activity Book**
Everything® Kids' Puzzle Book
Everything® Kids' Riddles & Brain Teasers Book
Everything® Kids' Science Experiments Book
Everything® Kids' Sharks Book
Everything® Kids' Soccer Book
Everything® Kids' Travel Activity Book

## KIDS' STORY BOOKS

Everything® Fairy Tales Book

## LANGUAGE

**Everything® Conversational Chinese Book with CD, $19.95**
Everything® Conversational Japanese Book with CD, $19.95
Everything® French Grammar Book
Everything® French Phrase Book, $9.95
Everything® French Verb Book, $9.95
Everything® German Practice Book with CD, $19.95
Everything® Inglés Book
Everything® Learning French Book
Everything® Learning German Book
Everything® Learning Italian Book
Everything® Learning Latin Book
Everything® Learning Spanish Book
**Everything® Russian Practice Book with CD, $19.95**
Everything® Sign Language Book
Everything® Spanish Grammar Book
Everything® Spanish Phrase Book, $9.95
Everything® Spanish Practice Book with CD, $19.95
Everything® Spanish Verb Book, $9.95

## MUSIC

Everything® Drums Book with CD, $19.95
Everything® Guitar Book
Everything® Guitar Chords Book with CD, $19.95
Everything® Home Recording Book
**Everything® Music Theory Book with CD, $19.95**
Everything® Reading Music Book with CD, $19.95
Everything® Rock & Blues Guitar Book (with CD), $19.95
Everything® Songwriting Book

## NEW AGE

Everything® Astrology Book, 2nd Ed.
**Everything® Birthday Personology Book**
Everything® Dreams Book, 2nd Ed.
Everything® Love Signs Book, $9.95
Everything® Numerology Book
Everything® Paganism Book
Everything® Palmistry Book
Everything® Psychic Book
Everything® Reiki Book
**Everything® Sex Signs Book, $9.95**
**Everything® Tarot Book, 2nd Ed.**
Everything® Wicca and Witchcraft Book

## PARENTING

Everything® Baby Names Book, 2nd Ed.
Everything® Baby Shower Book
Everything® Baby's First Food Book
Everything® Baby's First Year Book
Everything® Birthing Book
Everything® Breastfeeding Book
Everything® Father-to-Be Book
Everything® Father's First Year Book
Everything® Get Ready for Baby Book
Everything® Get Your Baby to Sleep Book, $9.95
Everything® Getting Pregnant Book
**Everything® Guide to Raising a One-Year-Old**
**Everything® Guide to Raising a Two-Year-Old**
Everything® Homeschooling Book
Everything® Mother's First Year Book
Everything® Parent's Guide to Children and Divorce
Everything® Parent's Guide to Children with ADD/ADHD
Everything® Parent's Guide to Children with Asperger's Syndrome
Everything® Parent's Guide to Children with Autism
Everything® Parent's Guide to Children with Bipolar Disorder
Everything® Parent's Guide to Children with Dyslexia
Everything® Parent's Guide to Positive Discipline
Everything® Parent's Guide to Raising a Successful Child
Everything® Parent's Guide to Raising Boys
Everything® Parent's Guide to Raising Siblings
**Everything® Parent's Guide to Sensory Integration Disorder**
Everything® Parent's Guide to Tantrums
Everything® Parent's Guide to the Overweight Child
Everything® Parent's Guide to the Strong-Willed Child
Everything® Parenting a Teenager Book
Everything® Potty Training Book, $9.95
Everything® Pregnancy Book, 2nd Ed.
Everything® Pregnancy Fitness Book
Everything® Pregnancy Nutrition Book
**Everything® Pregnancy Organizer, 2nd Ed., $16.95**
Everything® Toddler Activities Book
Everything® Toddler Book
Everything® Tween Book
Everything® Twins, Triplets, and More Book

## PETS

**Everything® Aquarium Book**
Everything® Boxer Book
Everything® Cat Book, 2nd Ed.
Everything® Chihuahua Book
Everything® Dachshund Book
Everything® Dog Book
Everything® Dog Health Book
**Everything® Dog Owner's Organizer, $16.95**
Everything® Dog Training and Tricks Book
Everything® German Shepherd Book
Everything® Golden Retriever Book
Everything® Horse Book
Everything® Horse Care Book
Everything® Horseback Riding Book
Everything® Labrador Retriever Book
Everything® Poodle Book
Everything® Pug Book
Everything® Puppy Book
Everything® Rottweiler Book
Everything® Small Dogs Book
Everything® Tropical Fish Book
Everything® Yorkshire Terrier Book

## REFERENCE

Everything® Blogging Book
**Everything® Build Your Vocabulary Book**
Everything® Car Care Book
Everything® Classical Mythology Book
Everything® Da Vinci Book
Everything® Divorce Book
Everything® Einstein Book
Everything® Etiquette Book, 2nd Ed.
Everything® Inventions and Patents Book
Everything® Mafia Book
Everything® Philosophy Book
Everything® Psychology Book
Everything® Shakespeare Book

## RELIGION

Everything® Angels Book
Everything® Bible Book
Everything® Buddhism Book
Everything® Catholicism Book
Everything® Christianity Book
Everything® History of the Bible Book
**Everything® Jesus Book**
Everything® Jewish History & Heritage Book
Everything® Judaism Book
Everything® Kabbalah Book
Everything® Koran Book
**Everything® Mary Book**

Everything® Mary Magdalene Book
Everything® Prayer Book
Everything® Saints Book
Everything® Torah Book
Everything® Understanding Islam Book
Everything® World's Religions Book
Everything® Zen Book

## SCHOOL & CAREERS

Everything® Alternative Careers Book
**Everything® Career Tests Book**
Everything® College Major Test Book
Everything® College Survival Book, 2nd Ed.
Everything® Cover Letter Book, 2nd Ed.
**Everything® Filmmaking Book**
Everything® Get-a-Job Book
Everything® Guide to Being a Paralegal
Everything® Guide to Being a Real Estate Agent
**Everything® Guide to Being a Sales Rep**
**Everything® Guide to Careers in Health Care**
**Everything® Guide to Careers in Law Enforcement**
**Everything® Guide to Government Jobs**
Everything® Guide to Starting and Running a Restaurant
Everything® Job Interview Book
Everything® New Nurse Book
Everything® New Teacher Book
Everything® Paying for College Book
Everything® Practice Interview Book
Everything® Resume Book, 2nd Ed.
Everything® Study Book

## SELF-HELP

Everything® Dating Book, 2nd Ed.
Everything® Great Sex Book
Everything® Kama Sutra Book
Everything® Self-Esteem Book

## SPORTS & FITNESS

**Everything® Easy Fitness Book**
Everything® Fishing Book
Everything® Golf Instruction Book
Everything® Pilates Book
Everything® Running Book
Everything® Weight Training Book
Everything® Yoga Book

## TRAVEL

Everything® Family Guide to Cruise Vacations
Everything® Family Guide to Hawaii

Everything® Family Guide to Las Vegas, 2nd Ed.
**Everything® Family Guide to Mexico**
Everything® Family Guide to New York City, 2nd Ed.
Everything® Family Guide to RV Travel & Campgrounds
Everything® Family Guide to the Caribbean
Everything® Family Guide to the Walt Disney World Resort®, Universal Studios®, and Greater Orlando, 4th Ed.
**Everything® Family Guide to Timeshares**
Everything® Family Guide to Washington D.C., 2nd Ed.
Everything® Guide to New England

## WEDDINGS

Everything® Bachelorette Party Book, $9.95
Everything® Bridesmaid Book, $9.95
**Everything® Destination Wedding Book**
Everything® Elopement Book, $9.95
Everything® Father of the Bride Book, $9.95
Everything® Groom Book, $9.95
Everything® Mother of the Bride Book, $9.95
Everything® Outdoor Wedding Book
Everything® Wedding Book, 3rd Ed.
Everything® Wedding Checklist, $9.95
Everything® Wedding Etiquette Book, $9.95
**Everything® Wedding Organizer, 2nd Ed., $16.95**
Everything® Wedding Shower Book, $9.95
Everything® Wedding Vows Book, $9.95
**Everything® Wedding Workout Book**
Everything® Weddings on a Budget Book, $9.95

## WRITING

Everything® Creative Writing Book
Everything® Get Published Book, 2nd Ed.
Everything® Grammar and Style Book
Everything® Guide to Writing a Book Proposal
Everything® Guide to Writing a Novel
Everything® Guide to Writing Children's Books
Everything® Guide to Writing Research Papers
Everything® Screenwriting Book
Everything® Writing Poetry Book
Everything® Writing Well Book